MODERN FURNITURE CLASSICS

MODERN FURNITURE

CLASSICS

MIRIAM STIMPSON

WHITNEY LIBRARY OF DESIGN
an imprint of Watson-Guptill Publications/New York

Dedicated to my colleagues and students in the Department of Design
at Brigham Young University and to my family and friends for their
constant enthusiasm and encouragement.

First published in 1987 in New York by Whitney Library of Design
an imprint of Watson-Guptill Publications
a division of Billboard Publications, Inc.
1515 Broadway, New York, NY 10036

Library of Congress Cataloging-in-Publication Data

Stimpson, Miriam F.
    Modern furniture classics. Pbk. ed.

    Bibliography: p.
    Includes index
    1. Furniture—History—19th century.   2. Furniture—
History—20th century.   3. Furniture—Styles.
I. Title
NK2385.S74   1987   749.2'049   87-2172
ISBN 0-8230-2969-7

Manufactured in U.S.A.

Paperback edition, first printing 1997

1 2 3 4 5 6 7 8 9 10 / 06 05 04 03 02 01 00 99 98 97

ACKNOWLEDGMENTS

I want to express special appreciation to the following people and organizations for photographs and invaluable information:

Linda Folland, Herman Miller, Inc., Michigan; Anna Casati, Cassina S.p.A., Italy; Joyce C. Clark and Heidi Hatfield, Knoll International, New York; Terry Kilwein, Furniture of the Twentieth Century, New York; Bard Henriksen, Fritz Hansen, Denmark; Debra De-Luca and Anna Ramsey, Atelier International, New York; Lorry Parks, Grace Designs, Texas; the staff at Thonet Industries, Pennsylvania; Susan Sweet, Art et Industrie, New York; Elaine Caldwell, Stendig, New York; Angela Georgiadis, ICF, New York; Barry Friedman, New York; Jordan-Volpe Gallery, New York; and to all the manufacturers, galleries, museums, and studios in the U.S.A., Europe, and Japan who provided material for this book.

Special thanks to Tina M. Jackson and Sally Sharp for their precise and engaging line drawings.

I am grateful to the many contemporary designers whose work is contained in this text for their time spent in interviews and personal correspondence.

Very special recognition is extended to Julia Moore, senior editor, and Victoria Craven-Cohn, associate editor, and the staff of the Whitney Library of Design for their professionalism, invaluable advice, attention to detail, and wholehearted support.

CONTENTS

PREFACE   9

THE BEGINNING OF MODERNISM   10

ARTS AND CRAFTS MOVEMENT   16

EARLY MODERNISM IN THE UNITED STATES   22

ART NOUVEAU   30

VIENNA SECESSION, WIENER WERKSTÄTTE, DEUTSCHER WERKBUND   44

MODERNISM IN HOLLAND   54

INTERNATIONAL STYLE AND BAUHAUS   60

ART DECO   74

THE 1930s   84

POSTWAR SCANDINAVIA   96

POSTWAR AMERICA   112

POSTWAR ITALY   128

POSTWAR GERMANY, FRANCE, ENGLAND, BRAZIL, MEXICO   142

THE 1970s   150

THE 1980s   166

DIRECTORIES   188

SELECTED BIBLIOGRAPHY   195

INDEX   197

CREDITS   204

PREFACE

This book presents the largest collection of modern furniture classics ever assembled in one volume—not only chairs and stools, but tables, sofas, lounges, chests, and wall units.

More than ever before, designers need the comprehensiveness of this approach in order to select the most appropriate furnishings for their clients. Likewise, students of design need to see the whole history of modern furniture—from its earliest beginnings to today—to gain mastery of this critical part of design history. Everyone, in fact, with an interest in modern design can benefit from this authoritative, illustrated survey, because *Modern Furniture Classics* makes it possible to appreciate and understand what is probably the most complete design expression of the modern idiom.

Modern Furniture Classics offers the material in a clear, convenient, and consistent format. The pieces are in a chronological and stylistic sequence. Although the focus of this book is on the piece, extensive supporting information about the designer, style, time period, design, country, manufacturer and distributor, and status of availability is provided to place each piece in a historical framework and to demonstrate patterns of design evolution.

Thousands of furnishings were examined and researched for this compilation. Pieces included in this book are those that have consistently emerged as classics of modern style.

The story of modern furniture begins in the wake of the Industrial Revolution, when furniture could be mass-produced in factories by machines instead of made by hand, piece by piece. Although for a long time a clear split between technology and art remained—new materials and inventions challenged the engineer, while designers were generally content to draw inspiration from past styles—the potential of technology was seen by a few forward-thinking designers.

Most important was the Austrian Michael Thonet, who produced what is considered to be the first modern furniture in the middle of the nineteenth century. After much experimenting, Thonet perfected a steam process for bending hardwood by machine, a process still used today. His furniture was first shown internationally at the London Exhibition of 1851, where it was appreciated immediately. Inexpensive and well-designed, bentwood chairs and other pieces became widely popular in Europe both for home and public use.

Thonet's company produced much of the world's classic modern furniture. In addition to Thonet's own designs, the company manufac-

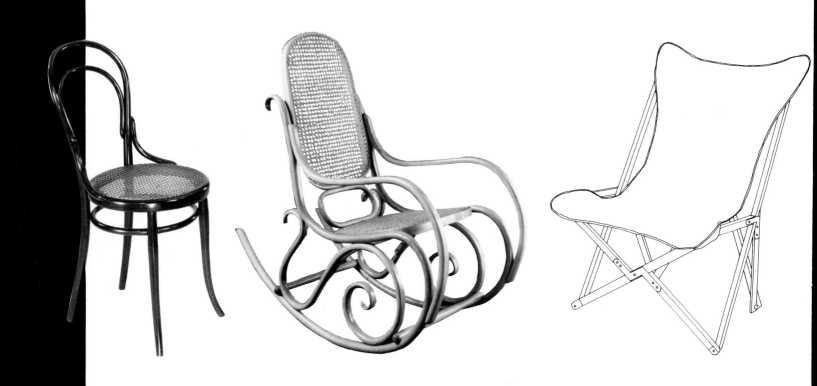

MODERNISM

tured some of the work of Josef Hoffmann and Otto Wagner, and later that of Mart Stam, Le Corbusier, and Bauhaus faculty members. It was the first company to make "knock-down" furniture and it shipped some chairs unassembled to both sides of the Atlantic. Thonet Industries still mass-produces modern classics by many designers.

Another early designer was Joseph Beverly Fenby, whose Tripolina Chair, created in 1877 of canvas and wood, was a simple and inexpensive provision of portable seating. The Colonial Chair (designer unknown) was another such innovation, also made of canvas and wood, but with a revolutionary structure, first used by British officers in India. Both chairs are still popular today. The Colonial Chair was updated by Denmark's Kaare Klint in 1933 and renamed the Safari Chair.

The Shakers in the United States were precursors of the modern movement. It was their idea, many decades before the Bauhaus, that form must follow function—one of the most important principles of modern design. Their furniture first became popular around 1860 and is popular again today.

CHAIR NO. 14, 1855

**DESIGNER: Michael Thonet
(1798–1871)
COUNTRY: Austria
STATUS: Mfr. by Thonet Industries
DIMENSIONS: W 17½" (44.6 cm),
D 22" (55.9 cm), H 34½" (87.8 cm)**

Michael Thonet did not invent bentwood furniture, but he perfected a process for mass-producing it. He opened his cabinetmaking business in 1819, in Boppard, Germany, and by 1840 he had developed the steam-softening method for bending rods of hardwood into flowing but structurally strong forms. His all-time classic, Model No. 14, has only six parts and ten screws. Thonet's process was much cheaper than the traditional methods of cutting, carving, and casting. At the turn of the century it sold for 75 cents. This chair, one of five similar designs, was widely copied after Thonet's patents expired in 1869, and more than 40 million chairs were sold by 1886.

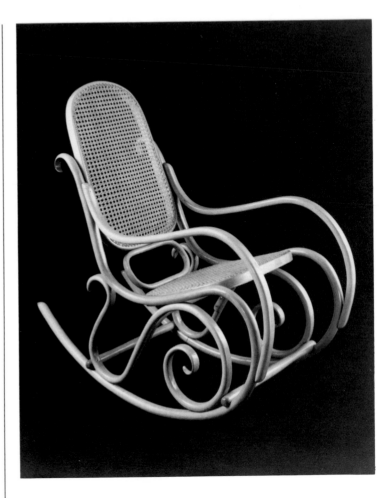

BENTWOOD ROCKER, 1860

**DESIGNER: Unknown
COUNTRY: Austria
STATUS: Mfr. by Thonet Industries
DIMENSIONS: W 21" (53.3 cm),
D 40" (101.6 cm), H 43" (109.2 cm)**

The Thonet Company, established by Thonet, made hundreds of variations of his bentwood designs, ranging from tables to coatracks. The company began manufacturing several similar styles of rockers in 1860, and soon it was making more than 100,000 a year. This one, with its swirling frame and natural cane seat, is similar in design to chairs made of wrought iron earlier in the century. It is light, durable, and inexpensive.

SHAKER FURNITURE, 1787–late nineteenth century

DESIGNERS: Shaker Craftsmen
COUNTRY: United States
STATUS: Reproductions by several mfrs.

A religious sect called the Shakers, founded in England in 1747, came to America in 1774, and founded their first community in 1787. The ascetic ideas of this group are clearly expressed in the clean, simple lines of the furniture they designed for their own use and later for sale to the public. Superbly crafted and devoid of "wicked decorations," because the Shakers believed that "beauty rests on utility," Shaker furniture was absolutely functional—embodying the form-function unity later adopted by the modern movement. Shaker furniture first became popular about 1860.

CORBUSIER CHAIR, circa 1904

DESIGNER: Unknown
COUNTRY: Austria
STATUS: Mfr. by Thonet Industries
**DIMENSIONS: W 21½″ (54.5 cm),
D 22½″ (57 cm), H 31″ (78.7 cm),
AH 27¾″ (70.4 cm)**

This lightweight classic bentwood chair, originally called the B-9 Chair, was nicknamed "Corbu Chair" for the architect who chose it for the living room of his pavilion in the Paris Exhibition of 1925 and other interiors. Le Corbusier said, "This chair, whose millions of representatives are used on the Continent and in the two Americas, possesses a nobility of its own." It is a distinctive chair.

COLONIAL CHAIR,
mid-nineteenth century

DESIGNER: Unknown
COUNTRY: England
STATUS: Not in production

The Colonial Chair (*left*) was designed for use by the British Army in India. Because it had to be portable, it had to be lightweight and it had to fold. In addition, it had to be able to withstand weather. Turned wooden elements held together by leather straps supported a leather or canvas seat and back. Tension in the construction allowed the chair to be stable on uneven terrain. Kaare Klint (1888–1954) of Denmark modified the Colonial Chair in 1933 and renamed it the Safari Chair (*right*). This chair is currently manufactured by Rud. Rasmussens Snedkerier.

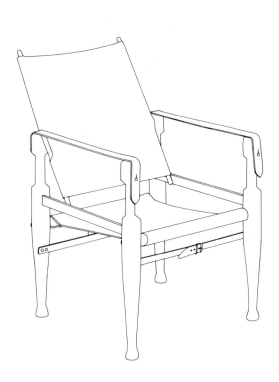

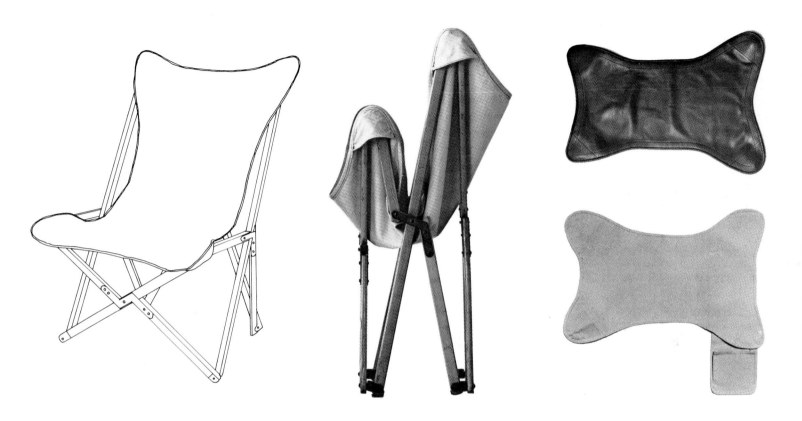

TRIPOLINA CHAIR,
circa 1855

DESIGNER: Joseph Beverly Fenby
COUNTRY: England
STATUS: Mfr. by Citterio
DIMENSIONS: W 30½" (77.5 cm),
D 30" (76.2 cm), H 39" (99.1 cm)

The popular Tripolina Chair was named and manufactured in Italy during the 1930s, but the inventor, Joseph Beverly Fenby, who designeed it around 1855, patented it in 1877. In the United States it was produced by the Gold Medal Company from the late nineteenth century, and both Thomas Edison and Theodore Roosevelt were known to have used it. It is made of wood and a canvas sling and folds compactly. The Butterfly Chair (page 95) designed by Hardoy, Bonet, and Kurchan is based on the Tripolina, though it has metal rather than wood supports.

ARTS AND CRAFTS

The modern movement in furniture began with the use of machines to mass-produce Michael Thonet's bentwood pieces, but the next important wave in the beginnings of modernism, the Arts and Crafts Movement in Great Britain, was a reaction against machine production. Inspired by the ideas of writer John Ruskin and the Pre-Raphaelites, the Arts and Crafts designers wanted a return to the deliberate craftsmanship and simple design of the Middle Ages. Artist and social reformer William Morris, the leader of the movement, believed that simplicity and fine craftsmanship were not possible in furniture made by machines. He and his followers formed Morris, Marshall & Faulkner—one of the world's first design firms—in 1861 to promote their anti-industrial philosophy. Their belief that good design should be essentially simple and available to all, regardless of social standing, as well as their concern for high-quality workmanship, became important modern principles.

MOVEMENT

One offshoot style important to the development of modern furniture was the Art Furniture Movement in Great Britain, which also flourished during the 1860s and 1870s. Charles Eastlake's popular book, *Hints on Household Taste in Furniture, Upholstery, and Other Details*, published in 1868, introduced the term *art furniture*. Unlike the purist Arts and Crafts designers, Art Furniture designers were convinced that machines could be used to produce fine, high-quality furniture.

The Arts and Crafts Movement in Great Britain led directly to other important developments in modern furniture, including Art Nouveau, the Deutscher Werkbund and the Vienna Secession, and the National Romantic Movement in Scandinavia. In the United States, it inspired the Mission Style, Prairie School, Arts and Crafts Movement, and the Craft Revival. In addition, crafts guilds, art museums, and other artistic societies were formed as a result of the Arts and Crafts Movement.

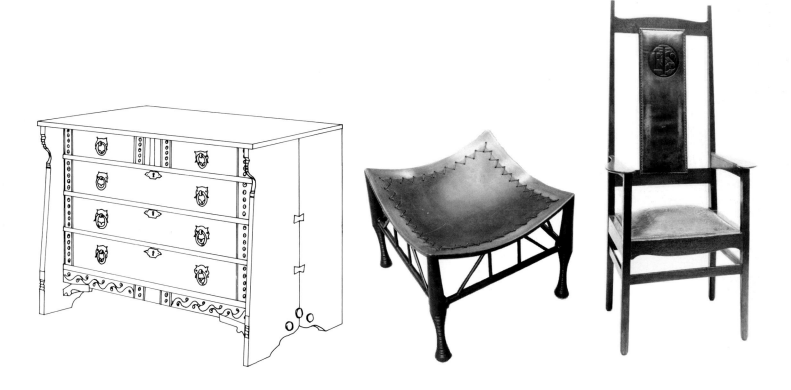

CABINET, 1861

DESIGNER: Philip Webb
(1831–1915)
STYLE: Arts and Crafts Movement
COUNTRY: England
STATUS: Not in production;
Collection, Victoria and
Albert Museum, London

Philip Webb was a leading member of the Arts and Crafts Movement. In addition to being an important architect, he was the chief furniture designer for William Morris's firm. Webb designed this oak cabinet, inspired by the medieval period, and Morris painted the panels depicting scenes from the legend of St. George. Both Webb and Morris felt this type of decoration was acceptable when "done for beauty's sake, and not for show." Although inspired by a style from the past, the design was simplified according to Arts and Crafts principles.

ARMCHAIR, circa 1865

DESIGNER: Philip Webb;
Often attributed to
William Morris (1834–1896)
STYLE: Arts and Crafts Movement
COUNTRY: England
STATUS: Not in production

One of many designs called the Morris Chair, this popular version, with its simple, honest construction, is a recognized symbol of the Arts and Crafts Movement. The various Morris chairs were probably designed by Philip Webb, based on an idea he got from a carpenter in Sussex. The chair has an adjustable solid wood frame and loose cushions for seat and back. It was widely copied, with many variations.

SIDEBOARD, circa 1867

DESIGNER: Edward William Godwin
(1833–1886)
STYLE: Art Furniture/
Anglo-Japanese
COUNTRY: England
STATUS: Not in production;
Collection, Victoria and
Albert Museum, London

After seeing Japanese works of art in the 1862 International Exhibition, E.W. Godwin redecorated his house in what he thought was Japanese style. Godwin's geometric approach is evident in this ebonized wood sideboard. He achieved this distinctive design effect by grouping solids and voids. The lightness, simplicity, and abstraction of his furniture influenced other designers—notably Charles Rennie Mackintosh in Scotland and Frank Lloyd Wright in the United States. Godwin's innovative furniture marked a significant break with historical revivalism popular during the latter part of the nineteenth century.

CHAIR, circa 1885

DESIGNER: Edward William Godwin
STYLE: Art Furniture/
Aesthetic Movement
COUNTRY: England
STATUS: Not in production;
Collection, Victoria and
Albert Museum, London

This ebonized oak chair, with legs like chair legs shown on ancient Greek vases, was typical of Godwin's continued concern with simplicity, lightness, and superb proportions.

By 1870, Godwin was a leading member of the Aesthetic Movement in England, which promoted lighter, less ornamental design, and yet he was well-grounded in the structural details of medieval furniture, as his notebooks show. Influenced by Charles Eastlake, Godwin designed houses, carpets, textiles, and wallpaper, as well as furniture. His designs were highly adaptable for factory production and were widely imitated.

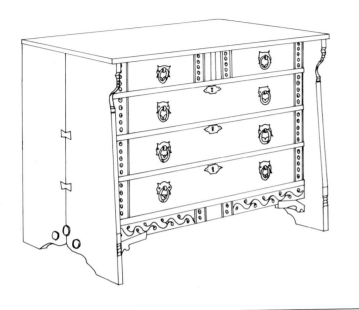

BEDROOM CHEST, 1868

DESIGNER: Charles L. Eastlake
(1836–1906)
STYLE: Arts and Crafts Movement/
Art Furniture
COUNTRY: England
STATUS: Never produced

Charles Eastlake, an important English architect, furniture designer, and author, became famous for his *Hints on Household Taste in Furniture, Upholstery and Other Details*, published in 1868. This popular book promoted simplicity and rectangularity of form, and honest craftsmanship. It helped make fussy early Victorian furniture passé. Inspired by Gothic ideals, this simple carved chest with handcrafted butterfly side joints was an illustration in Eastlake's book, the only piece never produced. He strongly felt that oak left in a natural state—not stained or varnished—was the proper wood for manufacturing furniture.

THEBES STOOL, 1884

DESIGNER: Leonard F. Wyburd
STYLE: Arts and Crafts Movement
STATUS: Not in production;
Collection, Victoria and
Albert Museum, London

Leonard Wyburd was the head of the Furnishings and Decoration Department at Liberty & Company, which was founded by Sir Arthur Lasenby Liberty (1843–1917). Liberty & Company still exists, with shops throughout England. It exported furnishings, fabrics, and accessories created by Arts and Crafts designers and, later, Art Nouveau designers. (In Italy, Art Nouveau is still known as Stile Liberty.) Influenced by an ancient Egyptian model, the Thebes Stool is made of walnut, mahogany, or oak, with a concave thonged leather seat and turned legs.

CHECKERBOARD CHEST,
late nineteenth century

**DESIGNER: Ernest Gimson
(1864–1919)
STYLE: Arts and Crafts Movement
COUNTRY: England
STATUS: Not in production**

Ernest Gimson was a prominent leader of the Arts and Crafts Movement after 1886. In 1895, he opened his own workshop in Cotswold, England, where he produced furniture free of historical detail and decoration, but with a feeling of the past incorporated into the design. The wood was treated to emphasize the beauty of its grain and often included elaborate marquetry and inlays of mother-of-pearl and ivory abstract or botanical motifs. Although he worked in textiles and also continued to practice architecture, Gimson is remembered for his handcrafted furniture, particularly chairs of turned ash with rush seats. This checkerboard chest, employing dramatically contrasting wood, is an excellent example of Gimson's work.

ARMCHAIR, circa 1907

**DESIGNER: Charles
Francis Annesley Voysey
(1857–1941)
STYLE: Arts and Crafts Movement
COUNTRY: England
STATUS: Not in production;
Collection, Victoria and
Albert Museum, London**

This handsome oak chair with distinctive leather back and seat was created for the Essex and Suffolk Insurance Company. (The embossed monogram is of the company's initials, *ESI*.) Voysey's domestic furnishings expressed the basic simplicity of joining individual pieces of wood to make sturdy forms. Opening his own office in 1882, Voysey was a principal exponent of the Arts and Crafts Movement although he did design some pieces for machine production.

EARLY MODERNISM

American designers in the second half of the nineteenth century were fascinated by the machine but, like William Morris, feared its social and political repercussions. For Americans, as for English designers of the time, Morris's desire for well-crafted simplicity as well as his interest in the medieval past had enormous influence.

The American Arts and Crafts Movement flourished from the late nineteenth century until 1916. A number of societies and guilds were formed with the goal of revitalizing and raising the aesthetic standards of furniture and other decorative arts. In New England, architect Henry Hobson Richardson was one of the first Americans to think that a building was not complete if the architect left the details and interiors to chance. He and the Herter brothers were influenced by the English Art Furniture works of A. W. N. Pugin, Charles Eastlake, and Richard Norman Shaw.

Gustav Stickley and Elbert Hubbard emerged

IN THE UNITED STATES

as two of the most prominent exponents of the crafts period on the Eastern Seaboard. Stickley's periodical, *The Craftsman*, first published in 1901, put forth Morris's philosophy and contributed greatly to popularizing it in the United States. Also influenced by the Arts and Crafts Movement, as well as by Oriental concepts and the work of Frank Lloyd Wright, Charles and Henry Greene of the California School created handcrafted furniture to harmonize with their organic houses.

Other American architects felt the importance of the unity of furniture and building design. Frank Lloyd Wright, George Washington Maher, and George Grant Elmslie, the three great architects of the Prairie School, created furnishings that maintained a unity of design. Theirs are considered the first consciously original designs America produced. By the late 1880s, Mission Style furniture, influenced by the Prairie School as well as by Morris, began to appear.

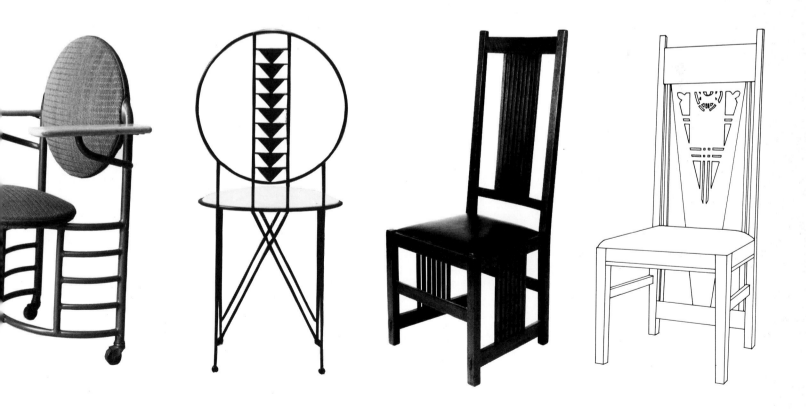

CATHEDRA CHAIR, 1869

DESIGNER: Henry Hobson
Richardson (1838–1886)
STYLE: Gothic/
Romanesque Revival
COUNTRY: United States
STATUS: Not in production;
Collection, Museum of Fine Arts,
Boston, gift of the Church of the
Unity-Unitarian Universalist

Many great architects during
the past century have created
furniture to complement their
buildings. Henry Hobson
Richardson, one of the first
architects to do so, was inspired in his work by the mas-
sive Gothic and Romanesque
cathedrals of Europe. The Cathedra Chair, designed for a
church interior and the first
piece of many that Richardson
designed for his own buildings, is an excellent example of
his Gothic/Romanesque style.
Reacting against the look of
machine-made pieces, he created handcrafted furniture in
full harmony with the ideals of
the Arts and Crafts Movement
in England.

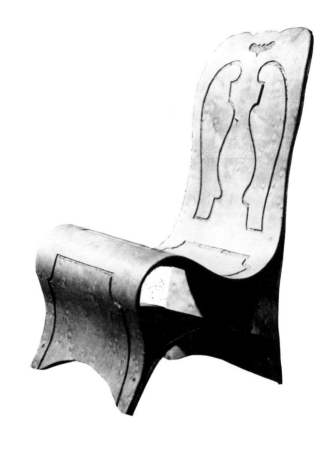

BENTWOOD CHAIR, 1873

DESIGNER: Sir Isaac Cole
STYLE: American Arts
and Crafts Movement
COUNTRY: United States
STATUS: Not in production;
Collection, The Museum of
Modern Art, New York

The process of bending wood
for furniture design was exploited in Boston as early as the
beginning of the nineteenth
century by Samuel Gragg
(1772–c. 1855). In 1808 he
patented his "elastic" plywood
chair. (Michael Thonet in Austria had perfected a process of
steam-bending rods of solid
wood by machine in 1855). In
1874, Isaac Cole created this
graceful curving chair made of
two lengths of molded plywood
bent by steam.

ARMCHAIR, 1903

DESIGNER: Harvey Ellis
(1852–1904)
STYLE: American Arts
and Crafts Movement
COUNTRY: United States
STATUS: Not in production;
Collection, Jordan-Volpe Gallery,
New York

Harvey Ellis's work was the link between that of Henry Hobson Richardson and Frank Lloyd Wright. After working as a draftsman for Richardson in Albany, New York, he returned to Rochester, where he was born, to practice architecture with his brother. He then lived a while in the Midwest, finally returning again to Rochester in the 1890s to design furniture for Gustav Stickley's Craftsman Workshops. He believed that "simple, structural plans, with an absence of applied ornament, are required for the construction of things made by hands." This armchair is beautifully executed in white quartersawn oak and is inlaid with copper, pewter, and secondary woods.

ARMCHAIR, 1907

DESIGNERS: Charles Sumner Greene
(1868–1957) and Henry Mather
Greene (1870–1954)
STYLE: American Arts
and Crafts Movement
COUNTRY: United States
STATUS: Not in production;
Collection, Gamble House,
Pasadena, California

Charles and Henry Greene practiced architecture primarily in Pasadena, California, from 1893. Inspired by Frank Lloyd Wright, the Arts and Crafts Movement in England, Stickley's *The Craftsman*, and Oriental concepts, these brothers developed a style of furniture that included rounded edges and raised pegs. Made of richly polished mahogany and walnut, their work was better crafted, more sophisticated, and more expensive than the contemporary and similar Mission Style furniture. This chair, designed for the Blacker House, is considered one of their finest pieces. Their architectural masterpiece, the Gamble House, also in Pasadena, is now a museum.

DINING CHAIRS, 1895

**DESIGNER: Frank Lloyd Wright
(1867–1959)
STYLE: Prairie School
COUNTRY: United States
STATUS: Not in production;
Collection, Wright Home and Studio
Foundation, Oak Park, Illinois**

Frank Lloyd Wright, one of America's greatest architects, believed that "a house must grow out of the land." His theories of organic architecture established a new direction, beginning with his conversion of the kitchen of his own house in Oak Park, Illinois, into a dining room. He wanted the furniture to form an integral unit with the architecture, and he created his own furniture to achieve this objective. These highback chairs are made of wood, with an emphasis on the vertical line to harmonize with the strong vertical lines of the dining room.

ROBIE CHAIR, 1908;
ALLEN TABLE, 1917

**DESIGNER: Frank Lloyd Wright
STYLE: Prairie School
COUNTRY: United States
STATUS: Mfr. by Cassina;
Dist. by Atelier International
DIMENSIONS: Robie:
W 15¾" (40 cm),
D 18" (45.7 cm), H 52½"
(133.4 cm)
Allen: W 110¼" (280 cm),
D 41¾" (106 cm)**

The Robie House, built in Chicago in 1909 for the F.C. Robie family, incorporates all the architectural characteristics of the Prairie School—a design approach developed by Frank Lloyd Wright in the late nineteenth century. It has high vertical back supports and provides a cozy and enveloping environment designed to harmonize with the strong horizontal lines of Prairie School architecture. The Allen table was designed for the Henry J. Allen house in Wichita, Kansas.

OFFICE ARMCHAIRS, 1904

DESIGNER: Frank Lloyd Wright
COUNTRY: United States
STATUS: Not in production;
Collection, The Museum of
Modern Art, New York,
gift of Edgar Kaufmann Jr.

In 1904, Wright introduced advanced office chairs constructed of metal with oak seats for the Larkin Company administration building in Buffalo, New York (destroyed by fire, 1950). Although in sympathy with William Morris's ideas about simplicity and fine craftsmanship, Wright believed the use of machines was vital for executing the pieces. He also believed in functional furniture and created steel file cabinets that could be stacked vertically and desks with attached legless chairs for easy maintenance.

MIDWAY CHAIR, 1914

DESIGNER: Frank Lloyd Wright
COUNTRY: United States
STATUS: Mfr. by Cassina;
Dist. by Atelier International
DIMENSIONS: W 15½" (39.4 cm),
D 18" (45.8 cm), H 34½" (87.6 cm)

The bright red Midway chair is geometrically designed with enameled steel rods. This chair, part of Wright's Midway Furniture Group, was created for the ill-fated Midway Gardens in Chicago—a beer restaurant doomed by Prohibition and destroyed before Repeal. The Midway Gardens project displayed a heavy use of sharply angled polygonal forms—a design incorporated into the compatible furniture.

SIDE CHAIR; SHIRTWAIST BOX, 1905

DESIGNER: Gustav Stickley (1857–1942)
STYLE: American Arts and Crafts Movement/Mission Style
COUNTRY: United States
STATUS: Not in production; Collection, Jordan-Volpe Gallery, New York

In 1898, Gustav Stickley, who had met Voysey and other designers in Europe, opened a furniture company near Syracuse, New York, to produce his simple, severe designs. By founding a periodical, *The Craftsman*, in 1901, he popularized his work and promoted the ideas of William Morris. His furniture, generally made of oak with exposed joinery, was sturdy and plain, without ornamentation. His chairs had canvas, rush, or leather seats. Called Mission Style furniture, the widely imitated originals bore Stickley's trademark, *The Craftsman*. Today they are collector's items.

LIBRARY TABLE, 1905

DESIGNER: George Washington Maher (1864–1926)
COUNTRY: United States
STYLE: Prairie School
STATUS: Not in production; Collection, The Art Institute of Chicago, Robert R. McCormick Charitable Trust

At age 13, George Washington Maher began to learn architecture in the Chicago firm where Frank Lloyd Wright and George Grant Elmslie worked. In 1888, Maher opened his own office in Chicago. For many residential commissions he used what he called the motif rhythm theory—drawing inspiration from the patron's interests for a linking design motif to achieve visual unity. Later, the Prairie School founded by Maher, Wright, and Elmslie in the 1890s used honest geometric shapes to achieve total unity of design.

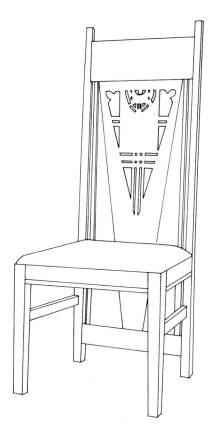

SIDE CHAIR, 1909

DESIGNER: George Grant Elmslie
(1871–1952)
STYLE: Prairie School
COUNTRY: United States
STATUS: Not in production;
Collection, The Art
Institute of Chicago

George Grant Elmslie was a Scot who came to America in the 1880s. He began to work in the Chicago firm of Joseph Lyman Silsbee, where he met both Frank Lloyd Wright and George Washington Maher. Later he joined Louis Sullivan's firm, staying for 20 years, until he joined with William Gray Purcell. Most of their work was residential, and Elmslie designed furniture fabrics and even landscapes for his homes, believing strongly in the need for total unity of design. This oak side chair was designed for the Charles A. Purcell House in Illinois.

ROYCROFTER FURNITURE, circa 1910

DESIGNER: Elbert Hubbard
(1856–1915)
STYLE: American Arts and Crafts
Movement/Mission Style
COUNTRY: United States
STATUS: Not in production;
Collection, Jordan-Volpe
Gallery, New York

Elbert Hubbard was a writer who retired with a fortune from his Larkin Soap Company to found the Roycrofters, a group of craftsmen, in East Aurora, New York. They produced metalwork, leatherwork, and heavy oak furniture—often with brass studs and leather seats—somewhat similar to Stickley's and also called Mission Style. Hubbard and his group adhered to the principles of William Morris and the Arts and Crafts Movement. This Roycrofter magazine stand is an excellent example of Hubbard's simplicity of design and fine craftsmanship.

ART NOUVEAU

When Samuel Bing opened his Paris shop, La Maison de l'Art Nouveau, in 1895, a new design style that had begun to appear about five years earlier was officially named. Bing had commissioned rooms by the Belgian architect and designer Henri van de Velde, as well as glass by Tiffany, posters by Beardsley, jewelry by Lalique, and sculpture by Rodin. The style caught on, becoming known as Jugendstil in Germany, Austria, and Scandinavia, Stile Liberty in Italy, and Modernismo in Spain. It was to remain popular only until 1910, but during its short ascendance, it dominated all the decorative arts, from posters to furniture.

Art Nouveau designers disclaimed any relationship with the past; however, some of their ideas have roots in the English Arts and Crafts Movement. Like earlier modern designers, Art Nouveau designers believed in unity of design.

All objects must be designed to fit the concept, down to the last interior and exterior detail.

Their inspiration came from nature. The lines of plants and the forms of birds and insects were the underpinnings of the most dominant form of Art Nouveau. Motifs included flowing patterns of plant stems and tendrils, seaweed, vines, and flowers like the iris, the rose, the lily pad, and the sunflower.

Designers also used ocean waves, swirling smoke, reptiles, peacocks, and swans. But perhaps most familiar of all was the motif of a slender, languorously posed woman with long flowing hair.

The rectilinear, geometric Art Nouveau style was more abstract than the flowing curvy one. It flourished especially in Scotland in the hands of Charles Rennie Mackintosh, and also in Vienna where it led to the Vienna Secession and the Wiener Werkstätte movements.

ARMCHAIR, 1898–1899

**DESIGNER: Henri van de Velde
(1863–1957)
STYLE: Art Nouveau
COUNTRY: Belgium
STATUS: Not in production;
Collection, Nordenfjeldske
Kunstindustrimuseum, Trondheim**

Trained as a painter and architect, Henri van de Velde, Art Nouveau's most ardent advocate, became a designer in order to combat ugliness in the world. In 1897, he formed the Société van de Velde, with workshops for furniture production and metalwork, and at the time he made many versions of this armchair. The flowing lines of the wooden frame are repeated in the stylized fabric. Van de Velde was very successful in Belgium, France, and Germany, designing many pieces for the wealthy and popularizing the Art Nouveau style for all.

SIDE CHAIR, 1896–1900

**DESIGNER: Victor Horta
(1861–1947)
STYLE: Art Nouveau
COUNTRY: Belgium
STATUS: Not in production;
Collection, Barry Friedman Ltd.,
New York**

The Belgian architect Victor Horta was one of the originators of Art Nouveau. His designs unified interiors and exteriors, subordinating and fusing many materials—cast iron, sculpted wood, stained glass, bronze, tiles—into an organic unity. In the famous stairhall of the Tassel House (1893), the stairway, the painted tendrils and the stair-rail all combine in an airy lightness of line that is reflected in his furniture. This chair, with its flowing forms and "whiplash" motif, is typical of Horta's approach. Brussels boasts many townhouses designed by Horta, and his own home is now a museum.

MUSIC CABINET FOR THE GRAND DUKE OF HESSE, circa 1898

DESIGNER: Mackay Hugh Baillie
Scott (1865–1945)
STYLE: Arts and Crafts
Movement/Art Nouveau
COUNTRY: England
STATUS: Not in production;
Collection, Victoria and
Albert Museum, London

Arts and Crafts architect and designer Baillie Scott designed this handsome cabinet for the Grand Duke of Hesse's palace at Darmstadt, Germany. The stylized flower and checker motifs were inspired by tapestries designed by Edward Burne-Jones, also an Arts and Crafts designer, but they are similar to Art Nouveau motifs. Like Art Nouveau designers, Baillie Scott believed that furniture must harmonize with the rooms it was in. From 1898, the furniture he designed—much of it for houses he also designed—was made by John White and sold by Liberty & Company.

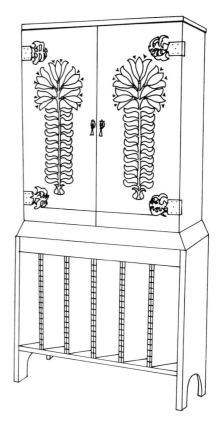

DINING CHAIR, circa 1882–1883

DESIGNER: Arthur Heygate
Mackmurdo (1851–1942)
STYLE: Arts and Crafts
Movement/Art Nouveau
COUNTRY: Great Britain
STATUS: Not in production;
Collection, Victoria and
Albert Museum, London

Although architect and designer Arthur Mackmurdo is primarily known as part of the Arts and Crafts Movement, his dining chair anticipated the Art Nouveau style by 10 years. It is mahogany with an upholstered seat, a swirling back, and painted decoration. Produced by Collinson & Lock in England, it was originally designed for the Century Guild, a crafts guild Mackmurdo founded with Selwyn Image in 1882. The Century Guild promoted the philosophy of the Arts and Crafts Movement and Art Nouveau.

SOFA FOR THE PARIS EXPOSITION, 1900

DESIGNER: Georges de Feure (1868–1928)
STYLE: Art Nouveau
COUNTRY: France
STATUS: Not in production; Collection, Danske Kunstindustrimuseet, Copenhagen

One of the most exquisite furnishings of the Art Nouveau period, this gilt ashwood sofa was created for the boudoir of Samuel Bing's Pavillon de l'Art Nouveau at the Paris Exposition in 1900—the design high point of the style. This feminine, luxurious, but refined sofa with delicately carved and gilt organic motifs is strongly reminiscent of eighteenth-century French sofa designs, despite Art Nouveau's claims of being totally ahistorical. The upholstery is embroidered silk, and the back of the sofa is a pair of butterfly's wings.

DESK, circa 1899

DESIGNER: Hector Guimard (1867–1942)
STYLE: Art Nouveau
COUNTRY: France
STATUS: Not in production; Collection, The Museum of Modern Art, New York, gift of Madame Hector Guimard

Hector Guimard was known for interpreting Art Nouveau in extreme terms. In strong, writhing forms, this desk, created for Guimard's own home, aptly expresses his devotion to the idea of an all-embracing, sinuous, organic environment. The combination of olive with ashwood panels emphasizes the lines of the piece. Guimard was an architect as well as a furniture designer. His works include not only the Métro entrances in Paris, but the Castel Béranger, a group of apartment houses in Paris, and many private residences.

CHAIR, 1902

DESIGNER: Emile Gallé
(1846–1904)
STYLE: Art Nouveau
COUNTRY: France
STATUS: Not in production;
Collection, Musée des Arts
Décoratifs, Paris

Gallé was an extraordinary French glassmaker who founded the prestigious School of Nancy in France. He became one of the leaders of the Art Nouveau style, creating furniture of curving organic forms, with structural elements deriving from specific plant or animal themes. Some details are carved in bas-relief with inlays of mother-of-pearl. Gallé was responsible for the revival of marquetry. He had a pictorial style using colors and grains of many different fruit-woods, incorporating inscriptions from Symbolist poetry as well as from flowers and insects. This chair is one of his finest pieces.

ARMCHAIR, 1900

DESIGNER: Louis Majorelle
(1859–1926)
STYLE: Art Nouveau
COUNTRY: France
STATUS: Not in production;
Collection, Barry Friedman Ltd.,
New York

Majorelle began his distinguished career designing furniture in his father's workshops in Nancy, France, reproducing popular eighteenth-century styles. By 1900, he had adopted the Art Nouveau style, becoming its main producer in France. His workshops were mechanized, and he produced luxury furniture in an organic style at prices the middle class could afford. This chair, made of walnut with tooled leather upholstery, is typical of his graceful, elegant approach to Art Nouveau, with its delicately carved ornamentation that seems to grow out of the form of the frame, emphasized by fabric in the same style.

ARMCHAIR, circa 1901–1902

DESIGNER: Antonio Gaudí (1852–1926)
STYLE: Art Nouveau (Modernismo)
COUNTRY: Spain
STATUS: Mfr. by B.D. Ediciones de Diseño
DIMENSIONS: W 25½" (65 cm), D 20½" (52 cm), H 37½" (95 cm)

Gaudí was labeled the wildest and most imaginative of all the Art Nouveau designers. He was an architect whose uninhibited, asymmetric furniture was meant for the buildings he designed. He had a penchant for scrolls, but his approach combined impulses of Gothic, Moorish, and other artistic traditions. This armchair was designed for the Casa Calvet in Barcelona. It is now made by B.D. Ediciones de Diseño of American oak carved with a hand gouge, finished with acid dyeing, and varnished with polyurethane.

CHAIR, circa 1900

DESIGNER: Hector Guimard
STYLE: Art Nouveau
COUNTRY: France
STATUS: Not in production; Collection, Musée des Arts Décoratifs, Paris

As one of the foremost Art Nouveau designers in France, Guimard's furniture was so popular it became known by supporters as the Style Guimard. The elusive interplay of organic forms and curves was hard to copy, but many tried. He used mostly pale woods, aiming for a harmony of design with sophisticated detail, and he was committed to an organic concept of the environment. He is perhaps best known for his delightful entrances to the Métro, Paris's subway: fanciful structures of cast iron.

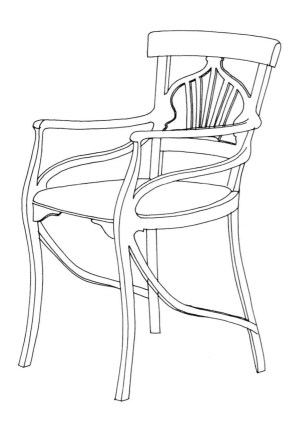

ARMCHAIR, circa 1898–1900

DESIGNERS: Ernesto Basile
(1857–1932) Vittorio Ducrot
STYLE: Art Nouveau (Stile Liberty)
COUNTRY: Italy
STATUS: Not in production

Ernesto Basile was the chief furniture designer in Vittorio Ducrot's workshop, where 200 people were employed. Active in architecture as well, the team designed several major works in the Stile Liberty, as Art Nouveau was known in Italy. This armchair, with its flowing forms and leather seat, was created for their Hotel Villa Igea in Palermo. Chairs designed by Basile and Ducrot for the Turin Exhibition of 1902 were mass-produced and very popular throughout Europe.

ARMCHAIR, 1895

DESIGNER: Carlo Bugatti
(1856–1940)
STYLE: Art Nouveau (Stile Liberty)
COUNTRY: Italy
STATUS: Not in production;
Collection, Barry
Friedman Ltd., New York

Bugatti is considered one of the most refreshing and original designers of the Art Nouveau period. He was a second-generation artist who painted and sculpted in addition to designing furniture. His extraordinary abstract insect forms, which showed traces of Japanese, Middle and Far Eastern, and Romanesque art, became increasingly dominated by the motif of the circle. This armchair, made of mahogany, ebonized mahogany, and inlaid with parchment, brass, pewter, ebony, and leather, is a good example of Bugatti's use of eighteenth-century form combined with a variety of motifs and contrasting materials.

ARGYLE CHAIR, 1897

DESIGNER: Charles Rennie
Mackintosh (1868–1928)
STYLE: Art Nouveau/Glasgow
COUNTRY: Scotland
STATUS: Mfr. by Cassina;
Dist. by Atelier International
DIMENSIONS: W 19" (48 cm),
D 18" (45.7 cm),
H 53½" (135.9 cm)

Scottish architect and designer
Charles Rennie Mackintosh
was one of the most important
Art Nouveau designers. In his
perpendicular style, he re-
garded the space around and
within his furniture to be as
essential to the design as the
upholstery or wood. This
stained oak Argyle Chair, the
first of many highback chairs,
has a stylized flying swallow
cutout and a seat that narrows
toward the back. It was created
for Miss Cranston's Argyle
Street Tea Rooms in Glasgow
—Miss Cranston was his foremost patron—and was also
used for dining in his own
home.

ARGYLE SET, 1897

DESIGNER: Charles Rennie
Mackintosh
STYLE: Art Nouveau/Glasgow
COUNTRY: Scotland
STATUS: Mfr. by Cassina;
Dist. by Atelier International
DIMENSIONS: W 25½" (65.3 cm),
D 25½" (65.3 cm), H 27" (68.5 cm)

While attending the Glasgow
School of Art, Mackintosh
formed a design group with his
future wife, Margaret Macdonald, her sister, Frances,
and Herbert MacNair. They
called themselves The Four
and were sometimes called The
Spooks by critics. They created
graphic works, especially posters, as well as daring interiors
and furniture in the perpendicular style of Art Nouveau.
The Argyle armchair and settee are of stained walnut on an
ebonized ashwood frame. The
fabric for the settee now produced is based on a characteristic Mackintosh rose motif,
designed by Margaret Mac-
donald, but the original had
plain horsehair upholstery.

PINK AND WHITE CHAIR, 1902

DESIGNER: Charles Rennie Mackintosh
STYLE: Art Nouveau/Glasgow
COUNTRY: Scotland
STATUS: Not in production; Collection, University of Glasgow

After creating furniture for his own home, Mackintosh designed pieces for the Glasgow School of Art (1897), private homes, and then commercially for the manufacturers Guthrie and Wells. Influenced by the colors in the paintings of James McNeill Whistler, he favored dark-stained or white-painted wood sparsely decorated with flower patterns in gemlike colors—patterns that look almost Japanese. When he combined straight lines with gentle curves as with this chair, his furniture had a fresh quality.

HILL HOUSE CHAIR I, 1903

DESIGNER: Charles Rennie Mackintosh
STYLE: Art Nouveau/Glasgow
COUNTRY: Scotland
STATUS: Mfr. by Cassina Dist. by Atelier International;
DIMENSIONS: W 16" (40.8 cm), D 15½" (39.1 cm), H 17½" (45 cm)

Mackintosh, with his inorganic use of wood, felt that design was more important than craftsmanship. This chair was designed for the white bedroom of Hill House. The original chair, which was painted white, was decorative and not meant to be sat upon.

HILL HOUSE CHAIR, 1904

DESIGNER: Charles Rennie Mackintosh
STYLE: Art Nouveau/Glasgow
COUNTRY: Scotland
STATUS: Mfr. by B.D. Ediciones de Diseño; Dist. by Furniture of the Twentieth Century
DIMENSIONS: W 16" (40.6 cm), D 16" (40.6 cm), H 44¾" (113.7 cm)

This highback chair of ebonized sycamore was designed for Mackintosh's Hill House, and was meant to be used with a writing desk. Its seat is upholstered in white linen.

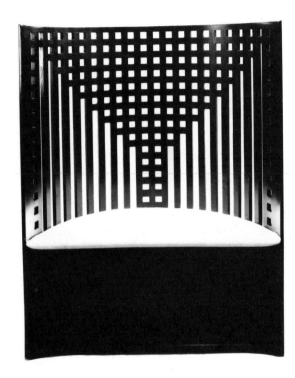

INGRAM STREET CHAIR, 1911

DESIGNER: Charles Rennie Mackintosh
STATUS: Mfr. by B.D. Ediciones de Diseño; Dist. by Furniture of the Twentieth Century
DIMENSIONS: W 15¼" (38.7 cm), D 16" (40.6 cm), H 32" (81.2 cm)

Created for the Ingram Street Tea Rooms in Glasgow, this chair was made of ebonized pine with a white linen seat. Its fretted back and side rails match the motifs of the Chinese Room there.

WILLOW I (CURVED LATTICE-BACK CHAIR), 1904

DESIGNER: Charles Rennie Mackintosh
STYLE: Art Nouveau/Glasgow
COUNTRY: Scotland
STATUS: Mfr. by Cassina; Dist. by Atelier International
DIMENSIONS: W 37" (94 cm), D 16.1" (40.9 cm), H 47" (119.1 cm), SH 15½" (39.6 cm)

This curved lattice-back chair was made for the order desk at Miss Cranston's Willow Tea Rooms where it acted as a room divider. In this chair, the supervisor took servers' orders and passed them down to the kitchen. Made of ebonized oak, with a segmental rather than semicircular form, the chair is remarkably high. Its checkerboard back—the lattice is made with insets between the verticals—forms a stylized tree pattern. The front of the seat opens to serve as a chest, and the bottom base curves out at the sides. Mackintosh also designed a similar but smaller chair called Willow II.

D.S. COLLECTION, 1918

DESIGNER: Charles Rennie
Mackintosh
STYLE: Art Nouveau/
Perpendicular/Glasgow
COUNTRY: Scotland
STATUS: Mfr. by Cassina;
Dist. by Atelier International
DIMENSIONS: Chair: W 19¼"
(48.9 cm), D 17¾" (45.1 cm),
H 29½" (74.9 cm)

This collection of pieces is based on drawings for dining room furniture for W. J. Bassett-Lowke or on a 1917 design for the Dug Out. It was not produced in Mackintosh's lifetime. Cassina began to make prototypes from the drawings, now in the collection of Glasgow University, in 1973, and has produced the furniture commercially since 1974. The D.S. Collection has strong geometric frames of ebonized ash or walnut-stained ash inlaid with mother-of-pearl. The chair seats are of sea grass. Two tables are available—one for dining and a smaller side table.

SIDE CHAIR, 1899

DESIGNER: Richard
Riemerschmid (1868–1957)
STYLE: Art Nouveau (Jugendstil)
COUNTRY: Germany
STATUS: Dist. by Jack Lenor Larsen
DIMENSIONS: W 23¼" (59 cm),
D 23¼" (59 cm), H 31" (79 cm),
SH 18" (45.7 cm),
AH 23½" (59.7 cm)

In addition to his affiliation with the Munich Secession group (Vereinigten Werkstätten für Kunst im Handwerk), architect Richard Riemerschmid was instrumental in establishing the Deutscher Werkbund in 1907, a design group that advocated good design for machine production. Riemerschmid was one of the first to make modern furniture for the masses in factories. This oak side chair with a leather seat displays Riemerschmid's elegance and simplicity of form, foreshadowing the Danish designs of Hans Wegner. It was designed for the Dresden Exhibition of 1899.

VITRINE, 1901

DESIGNER: Bernhard Pankok
(1872–1943)
STYLE: Art Nouveau (Jugendstil)
COUNTRY: Germany
STATUS: Not in production;
Collection, Kunstgewerbemuseum
Staatliche Museen Kulturbesitz,
West Berlin

Pankok's approach to furniture design was one of the most unusual interpretations of the Art Nouveau style. His heavy furniture often featured expressive butterfly wings splaying outward at the bottom of the pieces. This mahogany and cherrywood cabinet, created for the World Exhibition of 1904 in St. Louis, is one of Pankok's most important works. He was professionally active in Munich and Stuttgart, where he exerted much influence on Jugendstil artists.

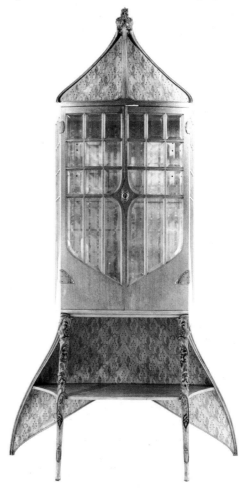

WHITE COLLECTION, circa 1910

DESIGNER: Eliel Saarinen
(1873–1950)
STYLE: Finnish National Romantic
COUNTRY: Finland
STATUS: Mfr. by ICF
DIMENSIONS: W 26¾" (67.9 cm),
D 21¼" (54 cm), H 32⅞"
(81.5 cm), SH 17¾" (45.1 cm),
AH 28⅜" (71.2 cm)

With Herman Gesellius and Armas Lindgren, Eliel Saarinen, the Finnish architect, designed his studio and living quarters, Hvitträsk, west of Helsinki (now open to the public). They also created exquisitely handcrafted furnishings in the National Romantic Style. Later Saarinen migrated to the United States, where he became director at Cranbrook Academy of Design Bloomfield Hills, Michigan. The White Collection, a superb example of National Romanticism, was designed for Saarinen's pergola at Hvitträsk. The carved solid beech frames are lacquered pearl white. The seats are covered with upholstery designed by Irma Kukkasjarvi.

ARMCHAIR, 1900

DESIGNER: Akseli Gallén-Kallela
(1865–1931)
STYLE: Finnish National Romantic
COUNTRY: Finland
STATUS: Not in production;
Collection, Museum für Kunst
und Gewerbe, Hamburg

This birch chair is an excellent example of the Finnish National Romantic Style, which was inspired by the ideas of William Morris and the Arts and Crafts Movement in England and by the Jugendstil in Germany and Austria. The shape of this chair, however, is Biedermeyer. A great promoter of National Romanticism, Gallén-Kallela was primarily a painter. With his friend Louis Sparre (1863–1964), he formed the Iris Company in 1897 in Porvoo, Finland, where he created simple handcrafted peasant furniture.

VIENNA SECESSION,

The Deutscher Werkbund (German Workshop) was founded in Munich by Hermann Muthesius (1861–1927) as a German equivalent of the Arts and Crafts Movement—but with an important difference: The designers and manufacturers of the Werkbund wanted to use machines to produce their work. Their goal was to create a serious standard for industrial design. Peter Behrens, Germany's first industrial designer, and Richard Riemerschmid—both important modern German architects—were the leading members of the Werkbund. The group's impressive exhibitions in Cologne in 1914 and in Stuttgart in 1927 had a tremendous influence on modernism.

Earlier, in 1892 in Munich, in 1898 in Vienna, and in 1899 in Berlin, there were a series of protests against the artistic establishment responsible for the pompous, historicist Ringstrasse style. Protesting groups of young designers and artists, including architects Otto Wagner, Adolf Loos, and Josef Hoffmann, were together

referred to as the Secession. They carved their philosophy over the door to Olbrich's Secession Gallery in Vienna: "To each time its art, to each art its freedom." Feeling strongly that artists must not be mired in past styles, they worked first in Jugendstil. Later their style evolved in a more geometric and structural direction, bringing art and design into the twentieth century.

The Wiener Werkstätte (Vienna Workshop) founded in 1903 by Josef Hoffmann and Koloman Moser, was an offshoot of the Secession movement. Designers worked in a studio setting to create handmade (and expensive) metalwork, furniture, and textiles in a remarkable style. They planned all the exterior and interior details of the Palais Stoclet in Brussels (1905–1911), a landmark of modern residential architecture.

The work of the Vienna Secession, the Werkbund, and the Wiener Werkstätte had a profound influence on the Bauhaus designers, Le Corbusier, and others who would further develop modernism in the coming decades.

POSTAL SAVINGS BANK STOOL, 1906

DESIGNER: Otto Wagner
COUNTRY: Austria
STYLE: Vienna Secession/
Wiener Werkstätte
STATUS: Not in production

Wagner's famous Postal Savings Bank showed a remarkable use of structural design for the times and was a distinct break from the Ringstrasse style favored in turn-of-the-century Vienna. This stool, designed for the main banking hall, had an ebonized finish, a perforated seat with cutout hand-hold, and aluminum details. Thonet Industries formerly reproduced it in elm veneer molded plywood with steam-bent elm legs.

POSTAL SAVINGS BANK ARMCHAIR, 1905–1906

DESIGNER: Otto Wagner
(1841–1918)
STYLE: Vienna Secession/
Wiener Werkstätte
COUNTRY: Austria
STATUS: Not in production;
Collection, Barry
Friedman Ltd., New York

Wagner was a founding member of the Vienna Secession. He taught at the Vienna Academy from 1894, where among his pupils were Josef Maria Olbrich, Josef Hoffmann, Adolf Loos, and Koloman Moser.

He was an architect who believed in staunch functionalism and the primacy of structure. For his Postal Savings Bank (1904–1906) he designed furniture that not only related to the exterior—both had aluminum detailing—but which also indicated, by the amount of metal on chairs and stools, the rank of the user. This beechwood stained armchair, based on an earlier design of Gustav Siegel, has a plywood seat and aluminum or brass shoes. It was formerly produced by Thonet Industries.

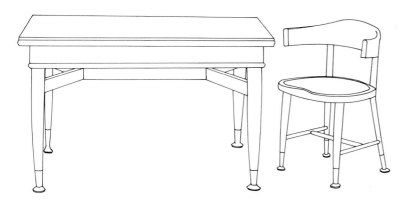

TABLE AND CHAIR, 1898

**DESIGNER: Adolf Loos
(1870–1933)
STYLE: Vienna Secession/
Wiener Werkstätte
COUNTRY: Austria
STATUS: Not in production**

One of the leaders of the Vienna Secession, Adolf Loos was known for his functional, austere interpretations of the style—although his work was less severe than his theory. Loos was a pioneering modern architect, and his Steiner House and Goldman & Salatsch Building caused much controversy in Vienna when they were built. This angular, functional chair and extendable table are made of mahogany with slightly tapered legs capped by bronze supports.

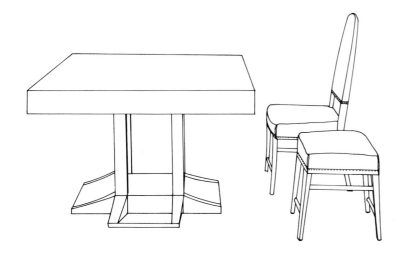

DARMSTADT FURNITURE SUITE, circa 1904

**DESIGNER: Josef Maria
Olbrich (1867–1908)
STYLE: Vienna Secession
COUNTRY: Austria
STATUS: Not in production**

Architect and designer Josef Maria Olbrich was a founding member of the Vienna Secession, and he designed the group's Secession Gallery. He was also a member of the Darmstadt Artists' Colony, founded by the Grand Duke of Hesse, for which he designed the communal studio and houses for artists, as well as much of the furniture. Like other modern designers, he was concerned with the total integration of furniture and building design. He favored abstract patterns and rounded shapes; his clearcut forms have little surface detail. This table, chair, and stool, designed for the music room in Darmstadt, became a prototype for modern style.

ROCKING CHAIR, 1905

DESIGNER: Josef Hoffmann
(1870–1956)
STYLE: Vienna Secession/
Wiener Werkstätte
COUNTRY: Austria
STATUS: Mfr. by ICF
DIMENSIONS: W 28¾" (73 cm),
D 50½" (128.3 cm), H 45½"
(115.6 cm), SH 18" (45.7 cm)

As a member of the avant-garde Vienna Secession from 1898 to 1903, Hoffmann created some of the world's most innovative furniture. In 1903, Hoffmann founded the Weiner Werkstätte, an offshoot of the Secession, and he continued to design furniture, metalwork, glass, and fabrics as well as to practice architecture. The Hoffmann Rocking Chair is constructed of bent beechwood lacquered black, with a contrasting seat and an adjustable ratcheted back. This chair is similar to another adjustable chair of Hoffmann's, called the Sitzmachine.

PURKERSDORF CHAIR, 1902

DESIGNER: Koloman Moser
(1868–1918); Often
attributed to Josef Hoffmann
STYLE: Vienna Secession
COUNTRY: Austria
STATUS: Mfr. by ICF
DIMENSIONS: W 24" (60.4 cm),
D 24" (60.4 cm), H 33" (83.8 cm),
SH 16½" (41.9 cm)

This painted beech chair was created for the main hall of the Purkersdorf Sanatorium in Vienna, an early modern work of extreme simplicity of Josef Hoffmann. Intended to be a part of a totally washable world, the wooden frames of the chair and the table that complements it have a white high-gloss finish. The seat of black and white webbing and the sophisticated black and white print of the fabric on the loose back cushion relate strikingly to the repeating verticals of the chair design.

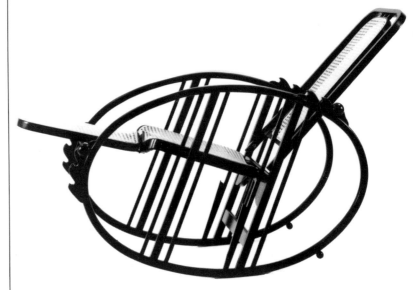

FLEDERMAUS CHAIR, 1907

DESIGNER: Josef Hoffmann
STYLE: Wiener Werkstätte
COUNTRY: Austria
STATUS: Mfr. by ICF
DIMENSIONS: W 19½" (49.5 cm),
D 18" (45.7 cm), H 30" (76.2 cm),
SH 18½" (47 cm)

This chair was created for a Viennese theater bar, modeled on cabarets in Munich and Paris, called Café Fledermaus. The lightweight frame of solid beech or elm is distinguished by short armrests and small ball forms which provide support under the seat. Originally manufactured by Jacob and Josef Kohn, the chair was painted black and white to match the cabaret room, but is now available in rosewood stain. A matching table is also available. The upholstery fabric shown here is based on motifs created by Charles Rennie Mackintosh—a designer Hoffmann admired greatly. The Fledermaus design is also available in a spindle-back side chair and settee.

ARMLÖFFEL CHAIR, 1908

DESIGNER: Josef Hoffmann
STYLE: Wiener Werkstätte
STATUS: Mfr. by ICF
DIMENSIONS: W 25¾" (65 cm),
D 19⅞" (50.5 cm),
H 37½" (95.1 cm)

The Armlöffel Chair is an excellent example of Hoffmann's rejection of romantic eclecticism. Its rectilinear frame, made of limed ebonized ash, reflects the influence of Charles Rennie Mackintosh. In 1900, Mackintosh and his wife, Margaret Macdonald, were invited to exhibit a tea room in the Vienna Secessionist Exhibition. Their work created a great deal of excitement on the Continent, and afterwards Mackintosh's influence was keenly felt. The Armlöffel Chair has a loose leather seat and spoon-shaped armrests.

PALAIS STOCLET CHAIR, 1905–1911

DESIGNER: Josef Hoffmann
STYLE: Wiener Werkstätte
COUNTRY: Austria
STATUS: Mfr. by ICF
DIMENSIONS: W 35½"
(90.1 cm), D 33½"
(85.1 cm), H 31½" (80 cm),
SH 17¾" (45.1 cm)

One of Hoffmann's greatest architectural achievements, the Palais Stoclet in Brussels, was designed in 1911 for the Stoclets, a wealthy family interested in promoting modernism. The structure established a new approach to residential design in Europe. Hoffmann and the Wiener Werkstätte designed the interiors, including all the furniture. This chair was meant for the great hall. The Werkstätte officially disbanded in 1932 because of financial difficulties. Recently there has been renewed interest in its work, and many furnishings have gone back into production.

KUBUS CHAIR, 1910

DESIGNER: Josef Hoffmann
STYLE: Wiener Werkstätte
COUNTRY: Austria
STATUS: Mfr. by ICF
DIMENSIONS: W 36" (91.4 cm),
D 30½" (77.5 cm), H 28½"
(72.4 cm), SH 17½" (44.6 cm)

The Kubus Chair is an early example of a structurally designed upholstered lounge chair. The Kubus is also available in two-seat and three-seat sofa sizes. Hoffmann used repeating cube forms, calling the chair "a study in perfect geometrics." The hardwood frame is covered with a rubber webbing and foam-upholstered leather. Hemispherical feet provide a contrast to the strong cube forms of the upholstered sections.

TWO-SEAT SOFA, 1913

DESIGNER: Josef Hoffmann
STYLE: Wiener Werkstätte
COUNTRY: Austria
STATUS: Mfr. by ICF
DIMENSIONS: W 54¾" (139.1 cm),
D 28½" (72.3 cm),
H 30¾" (78.1 cm)

This chair and sofa, designed for the Villa Gallia, expresses a design direction that would later be associated with the sophisticated Art Deco period of the 1920s and 1930s. They have wooden frames upholstered in a variety of single-color fabrics. Like the Haus Koller Chair, the Villa Gallia upholstery is highlighted with a distinctive contrasting outline. This design was typical of Hoffmann's output during the prewar period.

HAUS KOLLER CHAIR, 1911

DESIGNER: Josef Hoffmann
STYLE: Wiener Werkstätte
COUNTRY: Austria
STATUS: Mfr. by ICF
DIMENSIONS: W 35½" (90.1 cm),
D 32" (81.2 cm), H 37" (94 cm),
SH 16½" (41.9 cm),
AH 25½" (64.8 cm)

The Haus Koller Chair, named for Hoffmann's client, has a frame of hardwood with rubber webbing. Now made with foam-covered upholstery in black, brown, or rust with contrasting piping, it has a sunburst motif borrowed from ancient cultures. This motif was used later by Art Deco designers, and this chair is an important forerunner of that style. Two- and three-seat sofas in this design are also available. The two-seat size is 59" (149.9 cm) long, and the three-seat is 87½" (222.3 cm) long.

PRAGUE CHAIR, circa 1925

DESIGNER: Josef Hoffmann
STYLE: Vienna Secession/
Wiener Werkstätte
COUNTRY: Austria
STATUS: Dist. by Thonet Industries
DIMENSIONS: W 19¾" (50.2 cm),
D 20¾" (52.7 cm), H 31½"
(80 cm), SH 18½" (47 cm),
AH 27½" (69.9 cm)

The Prague Chair, designed in a stark, geometric, functional style, utilized the bentwood process developed by Michael Thonet. Thonet's company was the original manufacturer and still produces this chair in steam-bent elm with a cane seat. Now made in the United States and called the Hoffmann Chair, the frame is available with or without arms. Notice the differences in design from the Corbusier (B-9) Chair designed in 1904 (page 13).

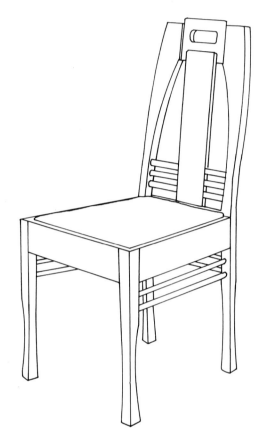

DINING CHAIR, 1902

DESIGNER: Peter Behrens
(1868–1940)
STYLE: Munich Secession/Darmstadt
COUNTRY: Germany
STATUS: Not in production

Peter Behrens was an architect and one of Germany's first industrial designers. Affiliated with the Munich Secession, the Darmstadt Artists' Colony, and the Deutscher Werkbund, his influence on the modern movement was significant, both in architecture and design. At the Prussian Academy in Berlin, Behrens had the opportunity to train three giants of modern architecture—Ludwig Mies van der Rohe, Walter Gropius, and Le Corbusier. Behrens's furniture was devoid of historical reference or detail, with simple shapes and clean proportions. This polished beechwood dining chair is a fine example of his work.

ARMCHAIR, circa 1911

DESIGNER: Hans Christiansen (1866–1945)
STYLE: Darmstadt
COUNTRY: Germany
STATUS: Not in production

Hans Christiansen was a painter and interior designer who became a member of the Darmstadt Artists' Colony in 1899. Influenced by the glass designs of Louis Tiffany, whose work he saw at the Chicago World Exhibition in 1893 as well as by the Darmstadt rectilinear style, he designed not only furniture, but also glass, ceramics, and jewelry—all with careful attention to craftsmanship. This armchair was made for Christiansen's home in Wiesbaden, to which he retired in 1911 to paint and write philosophy. Made of beechwood stained black, the chair is inlaid with Brazilian rosewood. Green, gray, and black striped fabric originally covered the seat.

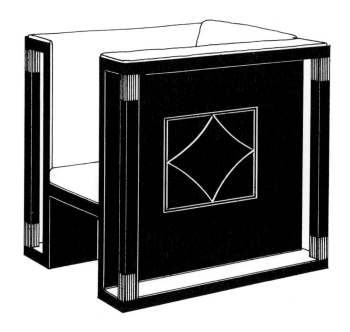

ARMCHAIR, 1904

DESIGNER: Koloman Moser
STYLE: Vienna Secession/ Wiener Werkstätte
COUNTRY: Austria
STATUS: Not in production

Moser was one of the principal founders of the Vienna Secession. He worked as an Art Nouveau painter and designer but later rejected floral ornament for a simpler, more austere style. In 1903, with Josef Hoffmann, Moser founded the Wiener Werkstätte—a more formal workshop organization that moved toward rectilinear forms. This angular armchair of veneered amboyna wood is accented with inlaid mother-of-pearl and other rich materials. Josef Urban (1872–1933) is another notable member of the Wiener Werkstätte. He emigrated to America in 1911, where he founded a sister branch of the Werkstätte in New York in 1922.

MODERNISM IN

Architect Hendrikus Petrus Berlage (1856–1934) brought the modern movement to Holland. His buildings and heavy, well-made furniture are clean, simple forms lacking in historical reference—features that were to become essential design principles.

In 1917 a radical art and design organization was founded in Leiden by painter Theo van Doesburg. De Stijl, as the group was called, included Piet Mondrian, J.J.P. Oud, and the great furniture designer and architect Gerrit Rietveld. Believing that "one serves mankind by enlightening it," they focused on spatial problems, adopting the Japanese qualities of austerity and sophistication, using straight lines and right angles and smooth, shiny surfaces. They hid

HOLLAND

wood grain with primary colors, plus black, white, and gray, and used no themes from nature. Their goal was to achieve harmony and balance in the home by limiting themselves to simple elements. They publicized their ideas, which they called neoplasticism, in their periodical *De Stijl*, in a lecture series, and through their projects and exhibits. Their influence on postwar designers was tremendous.

Although not a De Stijl member, architect Mart Stam was sympathetic to its values. He worked in Rotterdam developing his own ideas—among them the first cantilever chair. In the hands of Mies van der Rohe and Marcel Breuer, the cantilever chair became one of the totems by which modern furniture is known.

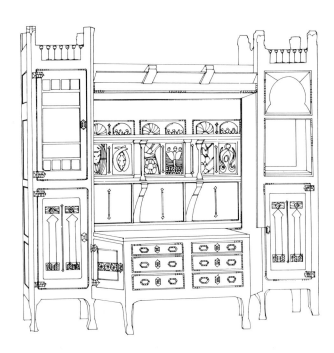

BUFFET, circa 1909

DESIGNER: Hendrikus Petrus
Berlage (1856–1934)
STYLE: Early Dutch Modern
COUNTRY: The Netherlands
STATUS: Not in production;
Collection, Gemeentemuseum,
The Hague

Early modern designer Hendrikus Petrus Berlage has been called the father of modern architecture in Holland.

His renowned Stock Exchange Building in Amsterdam (1898–1903), with its exposed red brick construction, remains an important landmark of the modern movement. Berlage's departure from historical detail is also evident in his furniture. A genuine concern for craftsmanship is expressed in this heavy oak buffet that depends on the bold use of structural members.

DINING SET,
early twentieth century

DESIGNER: Jacobus Johannes
Pieter Oud
STYLE: De Stijl
COUNTRY: The Netherlands
STATUS: Not in production

The architect J.J.P. Oud was a founding member of the De Stijl Movement in Holland. He designed the famous housing estate on the Hook of Holland and many other modern buildings in Rotterdam and gained worldwide attention. His furniture designs are based on the principles of the De Stijl group—simplicity of structure, geometric, angular forms, abstraction, and primary colors plus black, white, and gray. This beautifully simple dining set, for example, is constructed of blue-lacquered metal and black wood. This dining set was formerly manufactured by Ecart International and was distributed through Furniture of the Twentieth Century.

BUFFET, circa 1919

DESIGNER: Gerrit Rietveld
STYLE: De Stijl
COUNTRY: The Netherlands
STATUS: Not in production;
Collection, Stedelijk Museum,
Amsterdam

One of the leading members of the De Stijl Group in Holland was painter Piet Mondrian (1872–1944) whose abstract, rectilinear, primary-color paintings very much influenced the De Stijl architects and designers. Rietveld in particular was inspired by Mondrian's paintings, for example, in the creation of this sculptural buffet with its rhythmic use of straight lines and boxes.

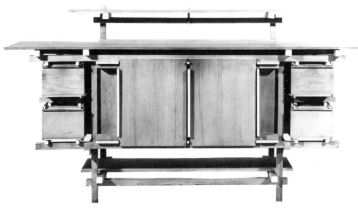

RED/BLUE CHAIR, 1918

DESIGNER: Gerrit Rietveld
(1888–1964)
STYLE: De Stijl
COUNTRY: The Netherlands
STATUS: Mfr. by Cassina;
Dist. by Atelier International
DIMENSIONS: W 26" (66.5 cm),
D 32½" (83.1 cm), H 34½"
(88.1 cm), SH 13" (33 cm)

Rietveld was not a member of the De Stijl group until after it featured this chair on the cover of *De Stijl*. The original chair had a natural wood finish, but later Rietveld painted it with red, blue, and yellow lacquer, and black aniline dye. He abandoned traditional joinery methods, using screws in order to have every member distinct from every other. Though it is surprisingly small, the Red/Blue Chair is an imposing, impressive piece of abstract sculpture and a seminal modern work.

SCHRÖDER TABLE, 1923

DESIGNER: Gerrit Rietveld
STYLE: De Stijl
COUNTRY: The Netherlands
STATUS: Mfr. by Cassina;
Dist. by Atelier International
DIMENSIONS: W 19½" (50 cm),
D 20¼" (51.6 cm),
H 23¾" (60.5 cm)

Rietveld's architectural master-piece was the Schröder House, built in 1924 in Utrecht. This table, made of particle board and plywood with a lacquered finish in red, white, black, yellow, and blue, was created to complement the Red/Blue Chair. It has a low square top and a unique sculptural two-part support column attached to a round base with beechwood dowels.

ZIGZAG CHAIR, 1934

DESIGNER: Gerrit Rietveld
STYLE: De Stijl
COUNTRY: The Netherlands
STATUS: Mfr. by Cassina;
Dist. by Atelier International
DIMENSIONS: W 14½" (37.1 cm),
D 17" (42.9 cm), H 29" (73.9 cm),
SH 17" (42.9 cm)

Rietveld wanted to construct a chair made out of one continu-ous piece of wood. However, he was forced to use four sepa-rate planes that had to be dove-tailed, glued, and bolted to withstand pressure. The Zig-zag Chair originally was made of untreated elmwood and was later lacquered in white with red or green edges.

BERLIN CHAIR, 1923

DESIGNER: Gerrit Rietveld
STYLE: De Stijl
COUNTRY: The Netherlands
STATUS: Not in production;
Collection, Stedelijk Museum,
Amsterdam

Rietveld was invited to plan a model room for the Berlin Ex-hibition in 1923—an exhibi-tion that was to feature the latest design developments from a number of countries. The simply constructed deal-wood Berlin Chair, lacquered white, light and dark gray, and black, was created for this ex-hibition. It was one of the world's first asymmetrical seat-ing units. Although few Berlin Chairs were actually produced, this De Stijl work was consid-ered one of the most exciting sculptural works of art of the time.

CRATE FURNITURE, 1934

DESIGNER: Gerrit Rietveld
STYLE: De Stijl
COUNTRY: The Netherlands
STATUS: Mfr. by Cassina
DIMENSIONS: Chair: W 21½"
(54.5 cm), D 23" (58.4 cm),
H 15¼" (38.7 cm)

During the Great Depression in Europe, Rietveld became interested in designing inexpensive furniture. He admired the well-built wooden crates used for shipping, and felt he could use it for chairs, tables, and bookshelves. He designed simple basic sections of unfinished boxwood to be screwed together by the purchaser. When the collection was first shown, it was criticized by those who didn't understand Rietveld's intentions.

S33 CHAIR, 1926

DESIGNER: Mart Stam (b. 1899)
STYLE: Early Dutch Modern
COUNTRY: The Netherlands
STATUS: Not in production

Mart Stam was the first designer to create a tubular steel cantilever chair. He designed the chair in 1924, but did not learn the techniques for bending steel until 1926. He met with Ludwig Mies van der Rohe and Marcel Breuer at a conference in Stuttgart to organize the Werkbund exhibition scheduled for 1927. Soon afterwards, Stam designed his S33 Chair, which was chrome-plated with a canvas seat. It was adapted for mass production by Thonet Industries. Mies and Breuer soon developed their own cantilevered chairs, the MR Chair (page 66), and the Cesca Chair (page 64).

INTERNATIONAL STYLE

During the time Josef Hoffmann and other members of the Wiener Werkstätte were working in Vienna, a center of modern design was growing in Germany. This was the Bauhaus—perhaps the design movement most associated with classic modern furniture. The Bauhaus, along with De Stijl, led to the development of the International Style, which was responsible for radically changing the urban environment in cities throughout the world. The Bauhaus did not spring from nowhere, of course. Like nearly every other development in modernism, some of the ideas and values it brought to bear on design came from William Morris. Like Morris, Bauhaus designers be-

lieved that their mission lay in improving society by making the environment harmonious and well-crafted. Unlike Morris, however, Bauhaus designers had nothing against the machine.

In 1904 the Belgian Art Nouveau designer Henri van de Velde was invited to become the director of the Weimar Art School and the School of Arts and Crafts. Walter Gropius was his successor, and Gropius renamed the school the Bauhaus in 1919. An impressive faculty was assembled, including Paul Klee, Wassily Kandinsky, Josef Albers, Lázló Maholy-Nagy, Marcel Breuer, and then later Mies van der Rohe. In 1925 the school moved to Dessau from Weimar; it flourished until 1933, when Hitler, who

AND BAUHAUS

perceived modernism as subversive, closed its doors forever.

Its purpose was not dissimilar to that of arts and crafts guilds already in existence: Its adherents wanted to design all of the built environment. While Arts and Crafts designers believed that good design should be available to all classes, because they avoided the machine (which they associated with inferior craftsmanship), their work, in practice, was available only to the wealthy. Designers of the Bauhaus saw the remedy in high-quality machine production; they sought to bring industry together with art in order to create prototypes for mass production, and they saw the need to develop new techniques and materials to make this possible. To do this, Walter Gropius planned a curriculum that included manual and technical training as well as intellectual training for all students.

The Shakers in the United States were among the first furniture designers who believed that function should be the determinant of form in design and that decorative detail served no useful purpose. Louis Sullivan, the architect who trained Frank Lloyd Wright, declared "form follows function" as his most important design principle. The Bauhaus adopted this principle because it legitimated simplicity, a return to basic abstract form in the tradition of De Stijl, and a concern for comfort and edification.

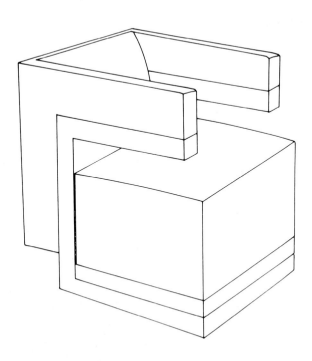

ARMCHAIR, 1924

DESIGNER: Marcel Breuer (1902–1981)
STYLE: Bauhaus
COUNTRY: Germany
STATUS: Not in production; Collection, The Museum of Modern Art, New York, Phyllis B. Lambert Fund

Breuer came to the Bauhaus to study at the age of 17. He was influenced by the ideas of Russian Constructivism as well as by those of De Stijl, and he designed light, simple, spacious furniture. His early chairs, like this oak armchair with woolen upholstery, reflect De Stijl influence, except that Breuer always had a concern for the sitter's comfort. Breuer became master of the Bauhaus woodwork and furniture workshops in 1925; there he developed the functional tubular steel designs for which he became famous.

ARMCHAIR, 1923

DESIGNER: Walter Gropius (1883–1969)
STYLE: Bauhaus
COUNTRY: Germany
STATUS: Not in production

The architect Walter Gropius was one of the most important leaders of the modern movement. First director of the Bauhaus, a school formed out of the merged Weimar Schools of Art and Arts and Crafts after World War I, Gropius shaped its aesthetic, advocating a unity of all the arts "which," he said, "will rise one day toward heaven from the hands of a million workers." This cherrywood armchair with lemon yellow upholstery, produced by students, follows his architectural principles. Its functionally different parts are obvious while the design retains its unity. Gropius came to the United States when World War II began, joining the faculty at Harvard's School of Architecture and popularizing Bauhaus ideas in America.

WASSILY CHAIR, 1925

DESIGNER: Marcel Breuer
STYLE: Bauhaus
COUNTRY: Germany
STATUS: Mfr. by Knoll International
DIMENSIONS: W 30¾" (78.1 cm),
D 27" (68.5 cm), H 28½"
(72.4 cm), SH 17" (42.8 cm)

Breuer was not the first to use tubular steel for indoor furniture. It had been used for children's beds and rocking chairs in the nineteenth century, although Breuer got the idea from his bicycle handlebars. The original Wassily Chair was bolted together, rather than welded as today, precluding total machine production. An ingenious use of Eisengarn fabric (now cowhide) for seat, back, and arms prevent the sitter from coming into contact with cold metal. Originally nickel plated (now chrome plated) with capped and polished ends, the chair is a boxy but complex arrangement of planes. It was named for the German Expressionist painter Wassily Kandinsky.

SPOLETO CHAIR, 1928

DESIGNER: Marcel Breuer
STYLE: Bauhaus/International
COUNTRY: Germany
STATUS: Mfr. by Knoll International
DIMENSIONS: W 18¼" (46.4 cm),
D 25⅜" (64.5 cm), H 30" (76.2 cm)

The Spoleto Chair was designed while Marcel Breuer was associated with the Bauhaus in Dessau, Germany.

This cantilevered chair has a frame of tubular steel finished in polished chrome. A remarkably similar design to Mart Stam's Chair S33 (page 59) designed in 1926, the Spoleto Chair is distinctive because of the exposed lacings on the back and the underside of the seat. These coverings are made of double-faced cowhide or reinforced canvas.

LOUNGE CHAIR, 1929

DESIGNER: Marcel Breuer
STYLE: Bauhaus
STATUS: Mfr. by Thonet
Industries and ICF
DIMENSIONS: W 22⅝" (57.5 cm),
D 22⅝" (57.5 cm), H 31¾"
(80.6 cm)

Breuer designed this innovative lounge chair while still at the Bauhaus. Because of the slope of the seat, the sitter's weight is placed toward the back of the chair, where it is most resilient. The springiness can also be felt in the cantilevered armrests, made of black lacquered wood. Seat and back materials come in a choice of wicker, leather, or pony skin. The lounge was produced for only a decade after it was designed. It was put back into production in 1973 and is still popular today.

CESCA CHAIR, 1928

DESIGNER: Marcel Breuer
STYLE: Bauhaus
COUNTRY: Germany
STATUS: Mfr. by Thonet Industries
DIMENSIONS: Side chair: W 18¼"
(46.4 cm), D 22½" (57 cm), H 32"
(81.2 cm), SH 18¼" (46.4 cm);
Armchair: W 23" (58.4 cm),
D 22½" (57 cm), H 32" (81.2 cm),
AH 27" (68.5 cm)

Known popularly as the Breuer Chair, the Cesca, named for Marcel Breuer's daughter, is the classic cantilever chair. Although Mart Stam had designed one in 1926 (page 59), Breuer got the idea, it is said, from turning one of his stools on its side. The original was made from a single length of steel tubing with a seat made of ebony-stained bentwood and caning, but now many variations are available. The wood can be dark or natural-finish oak or beech; the seat and back can be upholstered, hand or machine caned; the armchair can have wood or upholstered armrests. Cesca has become the twentieth-century equivalent of Michael Thonet's No. 14 Chair (page 12)—omnipresent.

ISOKON LOUNGE CHAIR, circa 1935

DESIGNER: Marcel Breuer
STYLE: International
COUNTRY: England
STATUS: Mfr. by Windmill Furniture;
Dist. by Furniture of the
Twentieth Century
DIMENSIONS: W 24" (61 cm),
L 56" (142.3 cm),
H 34" (86.4 cm)

Breuer migrated from Berlin to London in 1935, where he developed molded plywood furniture for the Isokon Furniture Company. This sculptural chair, often compared to Alvar Aalto's bent plywood furniture (pages 90–91), has a laminated beech frame and a plywood seat. An upholstered version was also manufactured by Isokon in 1935; later Gavina and Knoll International also produced it. In 1936 Breuer came to the United States, where he joined Walter Gropius at Harvard.

ALUMINUM CHAIR, 1933

DESIGNER: Marcel Breuer
STYLE: International
COUNTRY: Germany
STATUS: Not in production;
Collection, The Museum of
Modern Art, New York,
gift of the designer

Breuer turned his attention more toward architecture after leaving the Bauhaus, although he continued to design innovative furniture. During the 1930s he developed some of the first mass-produced, molded plywood chairs and some of the first aluminum-frame chairs, of which this chair is an example. The seat and back of the chair are made of flat bars of aluminum split in the center and slightly bent for resiliency. Only the armrests are made of wood. This chair and related designs in the Aluminum Group won two first prizes in a competition for aluminum furniture design in Paris in 1933. Some models were manufactured in small quantities by a Swiss firm.

MR CHAIR, 1927

DESIGNER: Ludwig Mies
van der Rohe (1886–1969)
STYLE: International
COUNTRY: Germany
STATUS: Mfr. by Knoll International
DIMENSIONS: W 21″ (53.3 cm),
D 32½″ (82.6 cm), H 31″ (78.7 cm)

Soon after Mart Stam produced his S33 Chair (page 59), Mies van der Rohe, the great German architect associated with the Bauhaus, presented his own, at the Deutscher Werkbund Exhibition in 1927. Nickel plated (later chromed) tubular steel, ¹⁵/₁₆″ diameter in three sections which are doweled and screwed together, forms the frame. The leather or canvas seat and back are fastened behind with laces. In 1931, Mies designed a lounge version of MR Chair with a deeper frame. The sweeping curve of the legs in both chairs exploits the flexibility of steel and the resiliency of cantilevering.

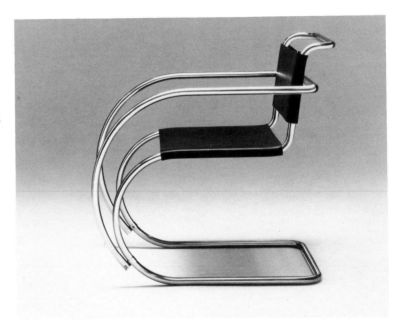

BRNO ARMCHAIR, 1929

DESIGNER: Ludwig Mies
van der Rohe
STYLE: Bauhaus/International
COUNTRY: Germany
STATUS: Mfr. by Knoll International
DIMENSIONS: W 23″ (58.4 cm),
D 23″ (58.4 cm), H 31½″
(80 cm), SH 17½″
(44.6 cm), AH 25¾″ (65.4 cm)

The Brno Chair was created for a dining table in the Tugendhat House in Brno, Czechoslovakia. The frame is made of chrome-plated flat bar steel—an innovative material that required quite a bit of hand finishing. The frame, with some structural changes, is now also available in tubular steel. The original was upholstered in leather, but fabrics are now available as well. Philip Johnson, the American architect, chose the flat bar version for the Four Seasons restaurant in New York City, making the chair a very popular contract furnishing. It has been mass-produced since 1960.

MR LOUNGES, 1931

DESIGNER: Ludwig Mies
van der Rohe
STYLE: Bauhaus
COUNTRY: Germany
STATUS: Mfr. by Knoll International
DIMENSIONS: Lounge: W 23⅝"
(60 cm), D 36¼" (92.1 cm),
H 33" (83.8 cm);
Chaise: W 23⅝" (60 cm), D 47¼"
(120 cm), H 37½" (95.3 cm)

The frames of these lounges are similar to the MR Chair frame—made of tubular steel sections doweled and screwed together. The cantilevered seat is supported by leather or rubber straps; the upholstery is padded and quilted in sections. The frames of these chairs are deeper and the seats more angled than on the MR Chair—increasing the comfort of the sitter. These chairs were manufactured first by Bamburg Metallwerkstätten, then by Thonet Industries, from 1932, and then reissued by Knoll International. Mies left Germany in 1938 to join the faculty of the Armour Institute (later known as the Illinois Institute of Technology) in Chicago, where he remained until he retired in 1958.

TUGENDHAT CHAIR, 1930

DESIGNER: Ludwig Mies van der Rohe
STYLE: International
COUNTRY: Germany
STATUS: Mfr. by Knoll International
DIMENSIONS: W 31" (78.7 cm), D 28" (71.1 cm), H 35" (88.9 cm)

The Tugendhat Chair, named for the family for whose house it was designed, combines the flexibility of the MR Chair with the richness of the Barcelona. Cantilevered for re-siliency, the Tugendhat's seat is very similar to the Barcelona's. Supported by leather straps, the cushion is welted, tufted, and (optionally) buttoned. The base is made of chrome-plated bar steel (now stainless), and the leg is S-shaped. Tugendhat is more comfortable than MR or Barcelona, and its popularity is perennial. There were many variations in the de-sign—Mies applied for 12 patents—but the original has always been the favorite.

BARCELONA CHAIR AND STOOL, 1929

DESIGNER: Ludwig Mies van der Rohe
STYLE: Bauhaus/International
COUNTRY: Germany
STATUS: Mfr. by Knoll International
DIMENSIONS: Chair: W 30" (76.2 cm), D 30" (76.2 cm), H 30" (76.2 cm), SH 17" (42.8 cm); Stool: W 23" (58.4 cm), D 22" (55.9 cm), H 14½" (36.8 cm)

Mies created this chair and stool for the German Pavilion at the Barcelona Exhibition of 1929. Originally made of chromed flat bar steel (now polished stainless steel), the bases of both use *cyma recta* curves—the chair has one; the stool, two—following the base shape of an ancient stool called *sella cirulis*. Surely Mies's finest furniture design, the pair require careful craftsmanship. The cushions are supported with leather straps, and the cushions themselves, which Lilly Reich helped Mies to design, are each made of 20 separate pieces of leather which are sewn together with welt-ing, biscuit-tufted, and buttoned.

COUCH; TUGENDHAT (BARCELONA) TABLE, 1930

DESIGNER: Ludwig Mies
van der Rohe
STYLE: International
COUNTRY: Germany
STATUS: Mfr. by Knoll International
DIMENSIONS: Couch: W 78"
(198.1 cm), D 39" (99.1 cm),
H 15½" (39.4 cm);
Table: W 40" (101.6 cm), D 40"
(101.6 cm), H 17" (42.8 cm)

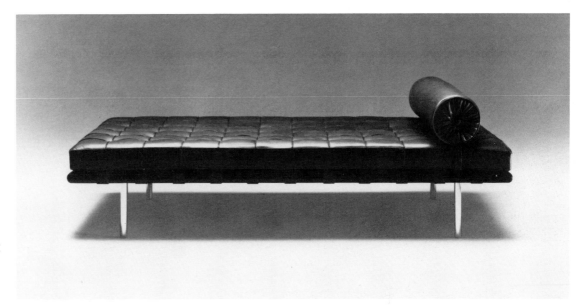

For the Barcelona Chair base Mies turned to an ancient stool design; for this couch, he turned to an ancient couch design—but using ancient forms, he created furniture wholly modern. The couch is the first to use both wood and metal for the frame—stainless steel legs are screwed into hardwood. The leather mattress (similar in design to the Barcelona Chair cushion) rests on rubber webbing; the bolster is strapped on. The table, usually erroneously called Barcelona, was designed for the Tugendhat House. Originally made of flat bar steel (now stainless), it has a joint-welded X-shaped base and a glass top. It has been mass-produced since 1948.

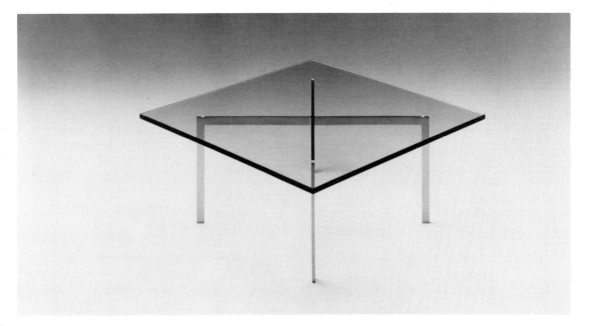

BASCULANT (LC-I) CHAIR, 1928

DESIGNER: Le Corbusier
(1887–1965)
STYLE: International
COUNTRY: France
STATUS: Mfr. by Cassina;
Dist. by Atelier International
DIMENSIONS: W 23½" (59.9 cm),
D 25½" (65 cm), H 25"
(64 cm), SH 15¾" (40 cm)

Le Corbusier (born Charles-Edouard Jeanneret, in Switzerland) was one of the most influential architects of the International Style; he is also famous for his furniture designs. He collaborated with his cousin Pierre Jeanneret and Charlotte Perriand to create this geometric machinelike chair using a welded frame of chrome or nickel-plated steel. Leather armrests loop like a conveyor belt over the tops of the turned leg tubes and the pivoting upholstery is held taut by tension springs. Although different in its exposure of all structural elements and its simplicity, the design was influenced by the Colonial Chair (page 14) and Breuer's Wassily Chair (page 63).

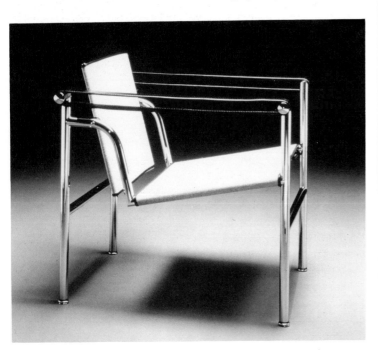

LC-2 PETIT CONFORT, 1928

DESIGNER: Le Corbusier
STYLE: International
COUNTRY: France
STATUS: Mfr. by Cassina;
Dist. by Atelier International
DIMENSIONS: W 30" (75.9 cm),
D 27½" (70.1 cm), H 26½"
(67.1 cm), SH 17" (42.9 cm)

Although influenced in this design by Hoffmann's Kubus Chair (page 50), Corbu did something new. He turned the armchair inside out. The structure of tubular metal forms a cage for the five down-stuffed (now foam) cushions, and exposed spring-held webbing forms the platform for the seat. Petit Confort is smaller, deeper, and higher than Grand, and the metal frame is available today in chrome or nickel plating as well as the original lacquer. As with Basculant, the Confort Chairs were the result of Corbu's collaboration with Perriand and Jeanneret.

LC-4 (PONY) CHAISE LOUNGE, 1928–1929

DESIGNER: Le Corbusier
STYLE: International
COUNTRY: France
STATUS: Mfr. by Cassina;
Dist. by Atelier International
DIMENSIONS: W 22¼" (56.4 cm),
D 63" (160 cm), H adjustable

With Charlotte Perriand, Le Corbusier designed this adjustable chaise, descended from the Thonet rocker of 1880, with runners of steel tubing resting on rubber-covered crossbars on a four-legged iron base. Originally the mattress, which snaps around the frame at the head and foot, rested on spring-held metal webbing, but since that abraded the pad, the webbing has been replaced with urethane framework. The bolster is held by a leather strap. Upholstery options include pony skin, leather, or fabric. It was designed for Corbu's Ville d'Avray in France and was first shown at the Salon d'Automne in Paris, in 1929, where it created a stir. Manufactured first by Thonet Industries, Cassina reintroduced it in 1965.

LC-7 (SIEGE TOURNANT) ARMCHAIR, 1928

DESIGNERS: Le Corbusier; Pierre Jeanneret; Charlotte Perriand
STYLE: International
COUNTRY: France
STATUS: Mfr. by Cassina;
Dist. by Atelier International
DIMENSIONS: W 23½" (59.9 cm),
D 33½" (84.8 cm), H 28¾"
(72.9 cm), SH 19¾" (50 cm)

The Siège Tournant introduced support springs as a base for the seat cushion; they radiate out from a central point like spokes on a wheel. The design for the arms is reminiscent of the Thonet B-9 Chair (page 13), which Le Corbusier had used for interiors. The seat revolves like an office chair. As in the Basculant and his chaise lounge, moving parts make reference to machines—an important part of Le Corbusier's idiom.

RECLINING LOUNGE CHAIR, 1929

**DESIGNER: René Herbst
(1891–1983)
STYLE: International
COUNTRY: France
STATUS: Mfr. by
formes nouvelles;
Dist. by J.G. Furniture Systems
DIMENSIONS: W 19″
(48.3 cm), L 34″–47″
(86.4 cm–94 cm), H 23″–41″
(58.4 cm–104.1 cm),
SH 12½″ (31.8 cm)**

René Herbst was one of the founders of the Union des Artistes Modernes in France. A leader of the functionalist aesthetic, he resisted excess decoration as did Le Corbusier, Eileen Gray, and Robert Mallet-Stevens. This chair is considered a classic piece for its innovation: made of Italian tubular steel painted black or nickel plated. The seat and back are washable cotton elastic straps in white or black.

TRANSAT CHAIR, 1927

**DESIGNER: Eileen Gray
(1879–1976)
STYLE: International/
French Modernist
COUNTRY: France
STATUS: Mfr. by Ecart International
Dist. by Furniture of the
Twentieth Century
DIMENSIONS: W 22″ (55.9 cm),
L 43″ (109.2 cm), H 31″ (78.8 cm)**

Born in England, Eileen Gray was trained as an architect, but she later opened a design workshop in Paris in 1922, where she created furniture, carpets, wall hangings, and screens. Her style began as a derivative of De Stijl and moved towards a stylish functionalism. She was especially famous for her lacquerwork. The Transat Chair has a padded leather seat, a frame of black or gray lacquered wood (or now, a natural ash) with chrome-plated metal details, and a pivoting backrest. The upholstery is leather or canvas. Gray was admired greatly by Corbu and other modern designers.

CHAIR, 1927

DESIGNER: Vladimir Tatlin
(1885–1953)
STYLE: International/
Russian Constructivist
COUNTRY: USSR
STATUS: Mfr. by Nikol International/
Delta Export
DIMENSIONS: W 23½″ (59.7 cm),
D 26″ (66.1 cm) H

The Russian Constructivist School of design, of which Vladimir Tatlin was a leading member, stressed the structure of objects rather than their aesthetic appeal. This chair, somewhat reminiscent of the Thonet B-9 Chair (page 13) combines cantilevering with a pedestal in an unusual design. Originally made of bentwood and caning, the frame is now made of tubular steel. The black leather cushion was inspired by the seat of a tractor.

STACKING CHAIR, 1928

DESIGNER: Attributed to Robert
Mallet-Stevens (1886–1945)
STYLE: International
COUNTRY: France
STATUS: Mfr. by Ecart International;
Dist. by Furniture of the
Twentieth Century
DIMENSIONS: W 17″ (43.2 cm)
D 16″ (40.6 cm), H 32″
(81.2 cm), SH 15¾″ (40 cm)

The fashionable French architect Robert Mallet-Stevens was a part of the Union des Artistes Modernes—a group that helped to bring the modern movement to France. Like Le Corbusier, Mallet-Stevens created furniture for buildings he designed. His designs were carefully crafted and expensive. This chair, which also stacks neatly, is considered one of his most successful. It comes in a semi-gloss gray, a black soft matte lacquer, and a high-gloss terracotta red.

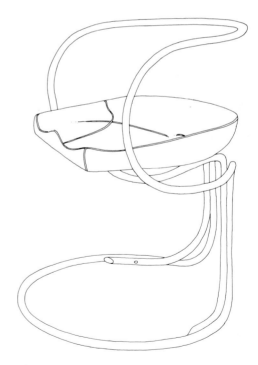

ART DECO

Though the International Style dominated much of European design during the years between the wars, another design movement, not wholly separate, but different in spirit, also flourished: Art Deco. French Moderne, as it was called to begin with, was the hit of l'Exposition des Arts Décoratifs in Paris in 1925. Unlike Bauhaus and International Style, Art Deco did not exploit the functional aspects of furnishings for design themes, and yet the style was "modernistic" rather than historical. Sleekness, streamlining, and an attention to geometry are important features of Art Deco pieces; they fit the environment of a world related to, if not wholly created by, the machine. Even in this nonfunctional style then, industry of the twentieth century made itself felt. This style could never have been the product of the nineteenth century.

And yet Art Deco (there is some dispute about when this term was coined: some say the 1960s, some say 1925) is rich in historical roots. For example, many themes were adopted from the ancient civilizations of Assyria, the Aztecs, and

Egypt (inspired by the opening of the tomb of Tutenkamen in 1922–1923). Other sources of inspiration were African art, Art Nouveau, Charles Rennie Mackintosh's works, the Wiener Werkstätte—especially Josef Hoffmann—and De Stijl.

Art Deco designers also borrowed contemporary ideas, as for example from the Bauhaus, as well as from popular culture: the iconography of transportation, of skyscrapers, of movies, of jazz. They made use of new materials. Not only tubular steel, but plastic, sharkskin (shagreen),

tinted glass, and frosted glass were all experimented with. They favored sophisticated colors like purple, mauve, peach, gray-green, turquoise, and brown, in addition to the De Stijl primary palette plus white, black, and gray. Shininess appealed to them; they lacquered or painted many pieces.

Art Deco became a fashionable revival style in the 1960s in the United States, and after fading a bit in the 1970s, resurfaced in the 1980s. Something perennial about the style allows it to be adapted again and again.

SERPENT CHAIR, circa 1912

DESIGNER: Eileen Gray
(1879–1976)
STYLE: French Moderne/Art Deco
COUNTRY: France
STATUS: Not in production

Some of Eileen Gray's work was done in the International Style (for example, the Transat Chair, page 72), but other pieces do not fit into that austere vocabulary. This chair, for example, which uses the playful element of snakes, is expressive rather than strictly functional. Gray was famous for her lacquer work; the serpent chair has an engraved red lacquer base and arms with a leather seat. She worked out of her own studio on the Rue du Faubourg Ste.-Honoré in Paris, designing textiles, screens, and store interiors, as well as practicing architecture.

ARMCHAIR, 1913

DESIGNER: Paul Iribe (1883–1935)
STYLE: French Moderne/Art Deco
COUNTRY: France
STATUS: Not in production;
Collection, Musée des Arts
Décoratifs, Paris

Even before World War I, as Art Nouveau was waning in popularity, Paul Iribe was developing a style that would help to define Art Deco. Iribe worked for Cecil B. DeMille and other Hollywood producers during the 1920s as a set designer. The drama of his work is evident in this mahogany chair upholstered in mauve silk. It is a good example of his work—generous in scale, even luxurious—with simple curves and proportions stressing its geometry.

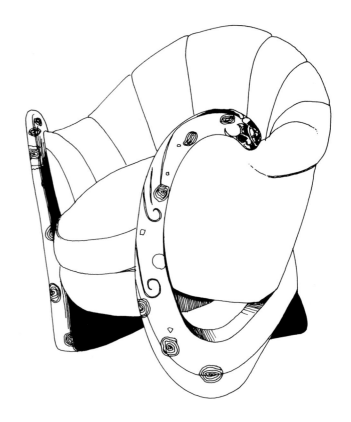

DESK AND FILE CABINET, 1918–1919; CHAIR, 1918–1928

DESIGNER: Jacques-Emile Ruhlmann (1879–1933)
STYLE: French Moderne/Art Deco
COUNTRY: France
STATUS: Not in production; Collection, The Metropolitan Museum of Art, New York, bequest of Collis P. Huntington

Soon after World War I, Ruhlmann, one of the most fashionable French Art Deco cabinetmakers, opened an interiors firm with M. Laurent. His formal furniture is characterized by refined neoclassical details and great craftsmanship. The chair shown here is upholstered in leather. Its tapered legs have silvered bronze shoes. The desk and file cabinet handles are made of ivory, as is the decorative motif. Ruhlmann elsewhere used sharkskin and leopardskin, ebony and amboyna woods, ivory details—all exotic materials, all expensive. His furniture maintains elegance despite its massiveness. It was very popular.

CABINET, 1922

DESIGNER: Jacques-Emile Ruhlmann
STYLE: French Moderne/Art Deco
COUNTRY: France
STATUS: Not in production; Collection, Musée des Arts Décoratifs, Paris

Ruhlmann was a leader of the French Moderne movement, lending a luxurious elegance to the style, which influenced many other designers. This cabinet of rosewood with Macassar ebony veneer is a noteworthy piece. In its inlaid ivory details it is somewhat reminiscent of the work of Charles Rennie Mackintosh, although Ruhlmann's work is far from the Perpendicular or Glasgow Style in feeling.

SUNBURST CHAIR, 1921

DESIGNER: Clément Rousseau
STYLE: Art Deco
COUNTRY: France
STATUS: Not in production;
Collection, Musée des Arts
Décoratifs, Paris

Influenced by Ruhlmann, Rousseau's furniture is elegant and classical in feeling. This side chair of ebony upholstered in blue silk has a sharkskin back tinted pink, white, and green with ivory fillets. Rousseau was one of the first designers to revive the use of sharkskin in furniture. The legs of the chair taper delicately in ivory shoes, an opulent touch. Ruhlmann and Rousseau both designed for the wealthy, as these details and fine hand craftsmanship show.

SIDE DINING CHAIR, circa 1923

DESIGNERS: Louis Süe
(1875–1968);
André Mare (1887–1932)
STYLE: French Moderne/Art Deco
COUNTRY: France
STATUS: Not in production

Louis Süe was a painter and architect; André Mare was a painter. In 1919 they founded a firm of artists and designers from various disciplines to work together on interiors called the Compagnie des Arts Français. They produced architecture, furniture, sculpture, tapestries, and glass for shops and homes. Their furniture was costly, featuring highly polished carved woods sometimes inlaid with mother-of-pearl. This leather upholstered ebony dining chair has a round seat, cabriole legs, and a tapered back.

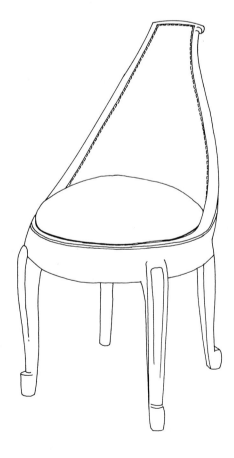

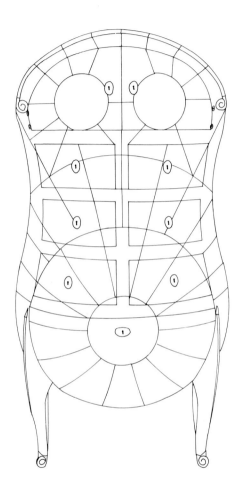

CABINET, circa 1925

DESIGNER: Jules-Emile Leleu (1883–1961)
STYLE: French Moderne/Art Deco
COUNTRY: France
STATUS: Not in production; Collection, The Metropolitan Museum of Art, New York, gift of Miss Agnes Miles Carpenter

A notable follower of Ruhlmann's elegant style, Leleu made furniture that was considerably less expensive.

He opened an interior design studio after World War I and by 1922 began to exhibit at major salons. He created a room for the 1925 Paris Exhibition, and many commissions followed. This cabinet—typical of his work—of amboyna wood is inlaid with a stylized flower motif in wood marquetry. Inlaid ivory outlines the piece and forms drawer handles and caps the bottom of the legs.

CHEST OF DRAWERS, 1923

DESIGNER: André Groult (1884–1967)
STYLE: French Moderne/Art Deco
COUNTRY: France
STATUS: Not in production

Like other French Moderne designers, André Groult took his inspiration from history—in this case, Louis Phillippe and Restoration furniture.

This rotund chest is a version of the eighteenth-century bombé chest, for example. In Groult's characteristic light wood, this piece is covered in sharkskin with ivory detailing. It was made for the Chambre de Madame in the Pavillon d'un Ambassadeur in the Paris Exhibition of 1925—a fair that did much to promote the modern movement.

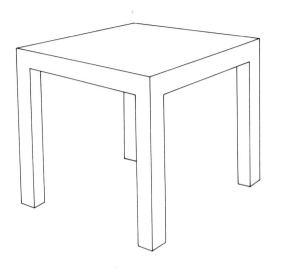

PARSONS TABLE, 1920s

DESIGNER: Jean-Michel Frank
COUNTRY: France
STYLE: Art Deco
STATUS: Mfr. by many companies

Perhaps originally designed by a Parisian, Jean-Michel Frank, to teach students perspective drawing at the Parsons School of Design in Paris, the Parsons Table, with its simple rectangular form, has become a staple item of modern furniture. Another theory credits the Russian Constructivist School with the first Parsons Table. It may have begun as a low occasional table; many variations in size and proportions have followed. Now most commonly made of plastic, or plastic laminate on wood, colors range through the spectrum, but black and white are the most popular.

CHAISE LOUNGE, circa 1925

DESIGNER: Pierre Legrain
(1889–1929)
STYLE: French Moderne/Art Deco
COUNTRY: France
STATUS: Not in production;
Collection, Musée des Arts
Décoratifs, Paris

Pierre Legrain studied with Paul Iribe after attending design school and afterwards collaborated with him on the interiors of couturier Jacques Doucet's apartment. Years later he designed Doucet's famous studio at Neuilly. His furniture combined unusual materials such as palm wood, vellum, zebra-patterned velvet, and lacquer with chunky proportions in a virile, confident style influenced by African art. This black lacquered, mother-of-pearl encrusted beechwood chaise is upholstered in zebra skin. In the 1920s Legrain created a glass and stainless steel piano—a famous, daring piece that was a total failure as an instrument.

CHAIR FOR THE IMPERIAL HOTEL, circa 1920

DESIGNER: Frank Lloyd Wright
STYLE: Art Deco
COUNTRY: United States
STATUS: Not in production;
Collection, Cooper-Hewitt Museum,
The Smithsonian Institution's
National Museum of Design,
gift of Tetsuzo Inumaru

Frank Lloyd Wright was commissioned by the emperor of Japan to design a hotel in Tokyo in 1914–1922. What he built was fantastic and extraordinary: the Imperial sent shock waves through the whole world of architecture. And when there was a major earthquake in Tokyo, the Imperial withstood it, not without shaking, but without any damage. Aztec motifs combined with Oriental themes informed the design, which was boldly geometric and classically palatial at the same time. This chair with an upholstered seat and back was designed to harmonize with the interior and exterior design.

COMBINATION DESK AND BOOKCASE, 1920s

DESIGNER: Paul Frankl
STYLE: Art Deco
COUNTRY: United States
STATUS: Not in production;
Collection, Grand Rapids
Art Museum,
gift of Dr. and Mrs. John Halick

After the Paris Exhibition of 1925 Americans began to take modern furniture more seriously. Paul Frankl, an American decorator, was very important in promoting it in the United States, realizing its potential for expressing the spirit of the times. Although the United States had not been invited to the Paris Exhibition, Frankl felt it had made a vital contribution to modern design in the form of the skyscraper. Why shouldn't furniture use this theme? This combination desk and bookcase is only one example of the series he created.

BLUE COLLECTION, 1929

DESIGNER: Eliel Saarinen
(1873–1950)
STYLE: Art Deco
COUNTRY: United States
STATUS: Mfr. by ICF
DIMENSIONS: Chair: W 25"
(63.5 cm), D 19¾" (50.2 cm),
H 30" (76.2 cm), SH 18" (45.7 cm)

In 1924, after winning second prize in the *Chicago Tribune* Tower competition in 1922, Eliel Saarinen and his family moved from Finland to Bloomfield Hills, Michigan, where he became the director of the Cranbrook Academy of Art. Saarinen directed the school through its golden age—when many innovative designers taught or trained there. He designed the Blue Collection for his wife Loja Gessellius's studio. Art Deco in style, the frames are made of beechwood lacquered blue-gray and highlighted with gold leaf. The seats are now foam filled and upholstered in Irma Kukkasjarvi's blue wool and nylon jacquard fabric.

SIDE CHAIR, 1929

DESIGNER: Eliel Saarinen
STYLE: Art Deco
COUNTRY: United States
STATUS: Mfr. by Arkitektura
DIMENSIONS: W 17" (42.8 cm),
D 19" (48.3 cm), H 37½"
(95.3 cm), SH 18" (45.7 cm)

Cranbrook Academy has recently licensed production of some of Eliel Saarinen's furniture designs for his own home in Michigan. (ICF also distributes some pieces.) The elegant Saarinen side chairs—only 13 of them were ever made—were designed to accompany an ornately inlaid round table. Arkitektura reproduces both table and chairs. The scalloped back of the maple chair was handcarved, with ebony and ocher enamel stripes.

SIDE TABLE, 1932

DESIGNER: Donald Deskey
STYLE: Art Deco
COUNTRY: United States
STATUS: Not in production

Radio City Music Hall (beautifully restored in the 1970s) is one of America's most famous showpieces of the Art Deco period. Interiors and furnishings were principally done by Donald Deskey, one of the best-known Art Deco furniture designers. Dazzling foyers and lounges, mezzanine, lobby, stairway, and theater all have murals, furniture, wallpaper, carpets, lighting, and metalwork in the sleek, sophisticated style. This table is made of painted wood and aluminum. It is one of Deskey's finest pieces. He also worked on other Art Deco projects in Rockefeller Center.

SMOKING TABLE, circa 1929

DESIGNER: Eileen Gray
STYLE: French Moderne/ International
COUNTRY: France
STATUS: Dist. by Stendig International
DIMENSIONS: Diameter: 20" (50.8 cm), H adjustable

By 1929, Eileen Gray became involved in total planning—creating buildings (she was a trained architect) and all the furnishings for them. Although some of her work was solidly Art Deco, she also designed in the International Style like her friend Le Corbusier. This sleek little table was designed by Gray with Jean Badovici for a house called E-1027 (from the magazine number it was published in) at Roqueburne. The tubular steel or brass stem on one side allows the table to be used as a bed tray for breakfast; the height of the glass top is adjustable. The small chain and the broken-circle base add visual interest.

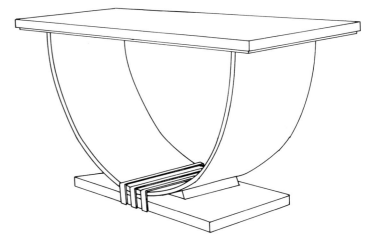

THE 1930s

In much of the Western world during the 1930s there was a Great Depression; many people were unemployed, many were poor. In Europe the economic instability was accompanied by political change: the Nazis came to power in Germany, and then annexed Austria; the Fascists came to power in Italy. Most styles of furniture design—from the Bauhaus and the International Style to Art Deco—were repressed. Yet there were stirrings of development in Italy, where the Fascists did not clamp down on designers as the Nazis did in Germany. In Scandinavia a reaction against the cold, machinelike precision of the International Style began to emerge. In the United States designers stuck to what was popu-

lar; the Art Deco style was rich in fantasy and nonfunctional ornament, meeting the needs of an impoverished nation in much the same way escapist Hollywood movies did.

In Italy Art Deco, the Italian Rationalist Movement, Futurism, and the Gruppo 7 were actively being developed by gifted Italian designers, including Giuseppe Terragni, Franco Albini, Gabriele Mucchi, Emanuele Rambaldi, and Gio Ponti. In addition to being a furniture designer, Ponti also started several magazines, including the beautifully produced *Domus*, to popularize designers' new ideas.

The International Style had spread throughout the world by the early thirties, and although

revered and widely adopted, it also had detractors. In Scandinavia, particularly, designers felt a lack of human warmth in its austere geometric, functional furniture made of glass and steel. Their traditional cultural values of family, nature, and home led them to design furniture that was surely influenced by International Style, but that was nevertheless warmer and more humane. The most famous Scandinavian designer of the period was Finland's Alvar Aalto. Others included for their importance are Bruno Mathsson, Erik Gunnar Asplund, Kaare Klint, and Mogens Koch.

In England the International Style held sway—in part because when the Bauhaus was closed by the Nazis, Marcel Breuer and Walter Gropius went to London. Gerald Summers worked in this style, creating most notably a bent plywood chair made from a single sheet. A different note was struck by the British-American T. H. Robsjohn-Gibbings, who created furniture based on ancient Greek themes.

Three others deserve to be mentioned: Salvador Dali, the Surrealist painter, who designed what may have been the first Pop Art furniture—the Mae West Sofa; the Argentines Hardoy, Kurchan, and Bonet, who transformed the Tripolina Chair into the Butterfly; and Hans Coray in Switzerland, whose stacking chair was the shape of much to come.

MONZA ARMCHAIR, 1930

DESIGNER: Giuseppe Terragni
(1904–1942)
STYLE: Italian Rationalist
COUNTRY: Italy
STATUS: Mfr. by Zanotta;
Dist. by Furniture of the
Twentieth Century
DIMENSIONS: W 27" (68.5 cm),
D 37¼" (94.6 cm), H 23½"
(59.7 cm), SH 14¼" (36.2 cm)

The sophisticated Italian design organization called Gruppo 7 was founded by Giuseppe Terragni, among others. He was an architect who worked in reaction to the austerity and flatness of the International Style—building Italy's first modern structures. He liked clean and simple forms such as this armchair, designed for Gruppo 7's Monza Exhibition. It has a black lacquered wood frame with gray cotton rep upholstery. Terragni is also well known for his Lariana or Follia Chair.

CHIAVARI CHAIR, 1933

DESIGNER: Emanuele Rambaldi
(b. 1900)
STYLE: Early Modern Italian
COUNTRY: Italy
STATUS: Not in production

The Chiavari Chair is named for the place where it was created by designer Emanuele Rambaldi—the Chiavari Workshop. This organization was established in the 1800s to produce simple, decorative furniture. The workshop was important in promoting modern Italian design. Made of maple with a woven seat and back, the Chiavari Chair was influenced by Bauhaus design.

GENNI LOUNGE CHAIR, 1935

DESIGNER: Gabriele Mucchi
(b. 1899)
STYLE: Italian Rationalist
STATUS: Mfr. by Zanotta;
Dist. by ICF
DIMENSIONS: W 22½" (57 cm),
D 43" (109.2 cm), H 30" (76.2 cm)
Ottoman: W 17¾" (45.1 cm),
D 21¾" (55.2 cm),
H 13¼" (33.7 cm)

The Italian Rationalists created furniture that exposed technical elements in a way not unlike some International Style designers. But their furniture was neither boxy nor austere. This chair, for example, by Gabriele Mucchi, a designer from Turin, is made of chrome-plated or fire-lacquered steel tubing with steel springs. The removable seat and headrest cushions are leather or fabric-covered polyurethane foam. The ottoman completes the design and adds considerably to the comfort of the sitter.

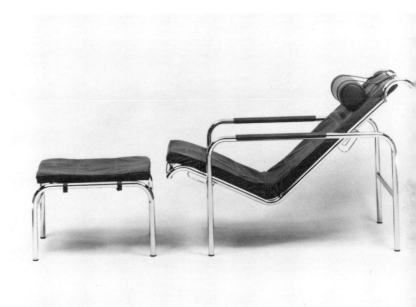

MAE WEST LIPS (MARILYN), 1936 (1972)

DESIGNER: Salvador Dali
(b. 1904)
STYLE: Surrealism
COUNTRY: Spain
STATUS: Dist. by Stendig
International (Marilyn)
DIMENSIONS: W 81" (205.7 cm),
D 33" (83.8 cm), H 34¾"
(88.3 cm), SH 16" (40.6 cm)

Salvador Dali created the Mae West Lips in a painting, and French designer Jean-Michel Frank had it made into a real piece of furniture for Baron de L'Epée and also for Edward James in London. The piece was named for the 1930s movie queen, of course, but when Studio 65 in Milan revived the design in 1972, it changed the name to that of an actress better known in the 1970s: Marilyn, for Marilyn Monroe. The Mae West had a seam across the lower lip, but Marilyn does not. The whimsical piece prefigures Pop Art; the humor of it prefigures that of Memphis—a 1980s Italian design group.

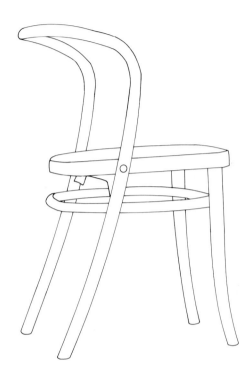

MK SAFARI CHAIR, 1933

DESIGNER: Mogens Koch (b. 1898)
STYLE: Early Danish Modern
COUNTRY: Denmark
STATUS: Mfr. by Rud.
Rasmussens Snedkerier
DIMENSIONS: W 21¾" (87 cm),
D 20¼" (52.1 cm), H 34½"
(87 cm), SH 14½" (36.8 cm)

Mogens Koch, who taught at the Royal Academy of Copenhagen, designed this Safari Chair in 1933, but it was not mass-produced until 1960, when Interna brought it out. Made of beech or rosewood with an unbleached flax or black oxhide seat and back, it is available in a child's size as well as an adult's. Now part of the permanent collection of the Victoria and Albert Museum in London, the Safari was first seen in the United States with the touring Arts of Denmark Exhibition in 1960. A matching table—made of a pearwood top on beech legs—was designed in 1960.

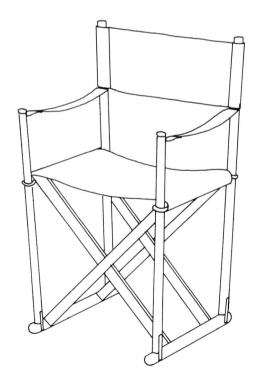

BENTWOOD CHAIR, 1930

DESIGNER: Søren Hansen
(b. 1905)
STYLE: Early Danish Modern
COUNTRY: Denmark
STATUS: Not in production

The first annual exhibition of the Copenhagen Cabinetmakers' Guild in 1927 was an event that acquainted the world with the high standards of Danish design. Excellent selection of materials, expert craftsmanship, and beauty of form are now well-known characteristics of Danish furniture. This bentwood chair, which is made by the Thonet process, was innovative in its time. Fritz Hansen, its former manufacturer (founded in 1872), promoted many new design ideas.

DECK CHAIR, 1933

DESIGNER: Kaare Klint
(1888–1954)
STYLE: Early Danish Modern
COUNTRY: Denmark
STATUS: Mfr. by Rud.
Rasmussens Snedkerier
DIMENSIONS: W 22½″ (57 cm),
D (extended) 57″ (144.8 cm),
H 35½″ (90.1 cm), SH 11″
(27.9 cm)

Kaare Klint taught at the
Danish Academy of Art from
1924, where he founded the
furniture department. As early
as 1916 he advocated sim-
plicity and functionalism in
furniture, and later made a
study of human anatomy and
physical activity in order to
improve the comfort and functional qualities of his furniture. He was one of the first
to use unvarnished wood and
natural fabrics—two ideas
Danish furniture is now famous for. This teakwood deck
chair, an update of a nine-
teenth-century design, with a
retractable footrest, is waxed
and polished.

BENT PLYWOOD ARMCHAIR, circa 1934

DESIGNER: Gerald Summers
STYLE: Early English Modern
COUNTRY: England
STATUS: Not in production;
Collection, Barry
Friedman Ltd., New York

This chair was the first to be
made from a single sheet of
plywood, requiring no assembly at all. Gerald Summers
developed it while working for
England's Simple Furniture
Company. It was lightweight
and therefore could be shipped
inexpensively; nevertheless,
not many were produced during the 1930s. Summers continued to work on bent
plywood and in 1938 created a
chair, little known outside pro-
fessional design circles, that
advanced the molding technique beyond the simple
curve, and paved the way for
Eames's later multiaxis work
(pages 114–117).

PENSION ARMCHAIR (406), 1935–1939

DESIGNER: Alvar Aalto
STYLE: Early Finnish Modern
COUNTRY: Finland
STATUS: Mfr. by Artek;
Dist. by ICF
DIMENSIONS: W 23⅜″ (60.7 cm),
D 28″ (71.1 cm), H 32¾″ (81.9 cm)

Aalto experimented for years with bent laminated wood and plywood, preferring birch. In this cantilevered armchair—a softer version of the Bauhaus style—the bent laminated birch frame supports a seat and back of webbing in neutral colors, black, or red. Webbing became popular in Scandinavian design—Bruno Mathsson used it often. Aalto, like Marcel Breuer, felt that humans should have to come in contact only with organic materials—(Breuer carefully designed the Wassily Chair [page 63] so that the sitter would never have to touch metal.)

PAIMIO CHAIR (41), 1931–1932

DESIGNER: Alvar Aalto
(1898–1976)
STYLE: Early Finnish Modern
COUNTRY: Finland
STATUS: Mfr. by Artek;
Dist. by ICF
DIMENSIONS: W 23⅜″ (59.4 cm),
D 31¼″ (79.4 cm),
H 24⅞″ (63.2 cm)

The greatest modern architect of Finland, Alvar Aalto, was also a great furniture designer. He designed this armchair while working on his famous early modern landmark, the tuberculosis sanatorium in Paimio, Finland—though the chair was not designed to be used there. It has a laminated birch frame with a molded plywood seat and back formed from one sheet of plywood into sinuous inverted scrolls. The arm-leg pieces are rigid, but the seat is resilient—this was one of the first such chairs to have no steel framework. Aalto designed a number of experimental versions of the chair over a three-year period.

STOOLS, 1932–1933

DESIGNER: Alvar Aalto
STYLE: Early Finnish Modern
COUNTRY: Finland
STATUS: Mfr. by Artek;
Dist. by ICF
DIMENSIONS: Various sizes
available

In his early years Aalto was inspired by Michael Thonet. He invented a way of making a structural support of laminated wood without a closed form. Aalto patented the technique, used first for this stool, which was used in Aalto's Viipuri Library. His tables and stools evolved over a long period and his later stools (page 98) are fanned at the join of leg to seat, unlike these. Aalto felt that "man's imagination must be given free rein," and that his experiments would lead to "useful forms."

TEA TROLLEY, 1935–1936

DESIGNER: Alvar Aalto
STYLE: Early Finnish Modern
COUNTRY: Finland
STATUS: Mfr. by Artek;
Dist. by ICF
DIMENSIONS: W 35" (88.9 cm),
D 19¾" (50.2 cm),
H 22¼" (56.5 cm)

Aalto is known for the way he combined the International Style with natural wood and humane values. Like many architects from Wright to Le Corbusier, Aalto considered his furniture designs to be essential for the completion of his architectural designs—calling them "accessories to architecture." In the late 1920s Aalto formed the Artek Company, along with his wife, Aino, and Mairea Gullichsen (for whom he had designed a villa), to produce his furniture. This tea cart was made by Artek of bent laminated frames with shelves of linoleum or tile. A large wheel dramatizes the functional form.

ARMCHAIR, 1936

DESIGNER: Alvar Aalto
STYLE: Early Finnish Modern
COUNTRY: Finland
STATUS: Mfr. by Artek
DIMENSIONS: W 21½" (54.5 cm),
D 30" (76.2 cm), H 23⅜" (59.4 cm)

The exposed laminated birch-wood cantilever frame of this armchair, designed by Aalto in 1936, supports a chunky up-holstered back and seat. When Aalto first designed a cantilever chair with a wood frame, in 1930, he used a steel support system for it. But the development of special glues and beech laminates allowed the metal to be dispensed with by 1936. Aalto's first all-wood cantilever chair, the Spring Leaf—not upholstered—was also produced in 1936.

SENNA CHAIR, 1925

DESIGNER: Erik Gunnar Asplund
(1885–1940)
STYLE: Classic Modernism
COUNTRY: Sweden
STATUS: Mfr. by Cassina;
Dist. by Atelier International
DIMENSIONS: W 36⅕" (91.9 cm),
D 45¼" (115.1 cm), H 44"
(111.8 cm)

Gunnar Asplund, born in Stockholm, was important in the development of modern Scandinavian architecture. He opened his own office in 1909; in 1930 he designed the buildings for the Werkbund Exhibition, bringing the International Style to Sweden. This lounge chair is made of walnut upholstered in beige, red, or black saddle leather with a silk-screened pattern. Armrests bear a decorative bas-relief. The chair is now produced under license by the architect's estate.

GOTEBORG I; GOTEBORG II, 1934–1937

DESIGNER: Erik Gunnar Asplund
COUNTRY: Sweden
STATUS: Mfr. by Cassina;
Dist. by Atelier International
DIMENSIONS: I: W 15.7″ (39.9 cm),
D 20.5″ (52.1 cm), H 31.5″ (80 cm);
II: W 29.9″ (75.9 cm), D 30.3″
(77 cm), H 34.5″ (87.6 cm)

Gunnar Asplund's Goteborg chairs demonstrate his clean, functional style in furniture—a Scandinavian version of the International Style, made warmer by the use of wood. Both chairs have natural wood frames of walnut or ash. Goteborg I (*left*) has an ABS seat and a self-supporting steel frame back upholstered with leather or fabric over polyurethane foam. Goteborg II (*right*) has a self-supporting leather seat and back. Both chairs are produced under license from the Asplund estate, as indicated by a signature and serial number found on each piece.

BARREL CHAIR, 1937

DESIGNER: Frank Lloyd Wright
COUNTRY: United States
STATUS: Mfr. by Cassina;
Dist. by Atelier International
DIMENSIONS: W 21½" (54.6 cm),
D 22½" (55.9 cm), H 31¼"
(79.4 cm)

Frank Lloyd Wright never abandoned his fascination with natural materials and never radically changed his aesthetic, despite his development toward furnishings more easily mass-produced. This chair, which was designed for Wing-spread, Herbert Johnson's Wisconsin house, is similar to an earlier design for the Martin House (1904). Made of solid cherrywood, this barrel chair uses a spindle-back design with a curved back. Wright felt that designing furniture for the houses he built was integral to designing the houses themselves.

KLISMOS CHAIR, 1936

DESIGNER: T.H. Robsjohn-Gibbings
(1905–1976)
COUNTRY: England/United States
STATUS: Mfr. by Saridis of Athens;
Dist. by Gretchen Bellinger
DIMENSIONS: W 20½" (52.1 cm),
D 18" (45.7 cm), H 35"
(88.9 cm), SH 17" (42.8 cm)

Writer, critic, and designer, T.H. Robsjohn-Gibbings attracted interest all over the world when he began to make furniture inspired by paintings on ancient Greek vases. The waxed birch Klismos Chair has a back constructed of three pieces of Greek walnut doweled together, with a woven leather-thong seat. The design owes much to a piece from the fifth century, B.C. Robsjohn-Gibbings was known for his humorous books, including *Mona Lisa's Mustache*, *Goodbye Mr. Chippendale*, and *Homes of the Brave*, in which he ridiculed the public's desperate quest to be in style.

BUTTERFLY CHAIR, 1938

DESIGNERS: Jorge Ferrari-Hardoy;
Juan Kurchan; Antonio Bonet
COUNTRY: Argentina
STATUS: Mfr. by many
manufacturers
DIMENSIONS: W 28″ (71.1 cm),
D 27¼″ (69.2 cm), H 35½″
(90.1 cm)

The inspiration for the Butterfly Chair came from the Tripolina Chair (page 15) used by British officers. Argentine architects Hardoy, Kurchan, and Bonet replaced the wood structure with one piece of bent steel; the seat is still canvas or leather. It slips onto the frame with inverted pockets to form a sling. At first manufactured by Knoll International, this tremendously popular and inexpensive chair has spawned many copies—more than five million to date.

LANDI STACKING CHAIR, 1939

DESIGNER: Hans Coray (b. 1906)
COUNTRY: Switzerland
STATUS: Mfr. by MEWA
P + W Blattmann
DIMENSIONS: W 20″ (50.8 cm),
D 24½″ (62.9 cm), H 30¼″
(76.8 cm), SH 16″ (40.6 cm)

Hans Coray developed this stacking chair at a time when steelhard tempered aluminum alloys were only beginning to be available. The innovative seat shell is formed of a single sheet of aluminum stamped by a press and punched with circular holes. An alkaline solution used to whiten the aluminum gives a distinctive crystalline appearance to the finish. Shown at the Swiss National Exhibition in 1938 as a chair suitable for outdoor use, the Landi has inspired a number of similar designs, including the Omkstack sheet metal chair by Rodney Kinsman (1974), made by Bieffeplast.

In the 1930s the emergence of Scandinavian design impressed the world. Aalto, Asplund, Mathsson, and Klint drew attention northward in Europe as they adapted and softened the International Style with Scandinavian traditional values. Exposed wood and fine craftsmanship, simple fabrics, and a sense of furniture as sculpture—these qualities were uniquely Scandinavian.

What made the furniture from Scandinavia during the 1940s and 1950s so special were the particular forms that the designs took. Alvar Aalto's innovative all-wood stools and tables were just the beginning. The development in Denmark of the Teak Style, as it was called, in the hands of Hans Wegner, Finn Juhl, Arne Jacobsen, Peter Hvidt, Børge Mogensen, and others, made the world take note. Wood was hand

finished, edges and corners were curved and smoothed, the fine craftsmanship showed—and was an integral part of the design.

Machine production was not forgotten. Later Scandinavians, like Eero Aarnio, Poul Kjaerholm, and Verner Panton all exploited machines for their designs. So did Yrjö Kukkapuro, Jørn Utzon, and Steen Ostergaard. And with the machine came a gradual change in the typical Scandinavian design silhouette—a change toward more organic, nonrectangular forms.

There was also a change in materials. As well as the Teak Style, Scandinavian furniture moved into another world altogether—not into the classical chromed steel of the Bauhaus, but into molded plastic and fiberglass and wire.

Developments in Scandinavia predicted much that was to come.

MATHSSON LOUNGE, circa 1940

DESIGNER: Bruno Mathsson (b. 1907)
STYLE: Swedish Modern
COUNTRY: Sweden
STATUS: Mfr. by Dux Möbel; Collection, Barry Friedman Ltd., New York
DIMENSIONS: W 23½″ (59.7 cm), D 27½″ (69.9 cm), H 40″ (101.6 cm), SH 12½″ (31.8 cm)

Bruno Mathsson made anatomy studies of the way people sit before he developed his bent plywood furniture. The legs of his chairs are flexible rather than rigid; for upholstery he used tightly woven webbing and upholstery. Both features enhance the sitter's comfort. Influenced by Asplund and Aalto, Mathsson experimented with several different kinds of seats and backs for his chairs. He often decided to separate the seat and frame elements. These chairs are made of laminated beech and webbing of leather strips. Mathsson worked in his father's firm, K. Mathsson, Värnamo.

STOOLS AND TABLES, 1954

DESIGNER: Alvar Aalto
STYLE: Finnish Modern
COUNTRY: Finland
STATUS: Mfr. by Artek; Dist. by ICF
DIMENSIONS: Variable

Alvar Aalto's design of the fanned wood structural support for these stools and tables typifies the sculptural approach he took to furniture. He experimented with molded wood over a long period of time and his methods evolved brilliantly. Aalto used no screws. The legs were backsawed and blended into the wood of the top or seat. This joint was invented by him to integrate the seat or top and legs completely. The beauty of these stools has made them popular.

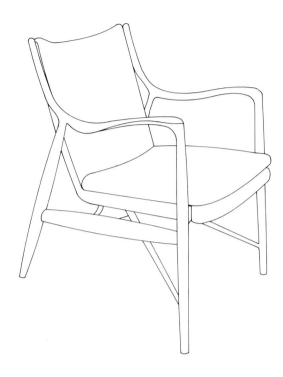

AX CHAIR, 1950

DESIGNER: Peter Hvidt (b. 1916)
STYLE: Danish Modern
COUNTRY: Denmark
STATUS: Not in production

The Ax group of chairs is made of laminated beech glued to teak or mahogany in a process (called lamella-gluing) developed by Peter Hvidt's firm, Hvidt and Mølgaard-Nielsen. This process was similar to that used in making tennis rackets. The frame is made of one piece attached to the back and seat with dowels. The seats are wood or padded and upholstered in either leather or fabric. The chair was made by Fritz Hansen and shipped unassembled.

EASY CHAIR, 1945

DESIGNER: Finn Juhl (b. 1912)
STYLE: Danish Modern
COUNTRY: Denmark
STATUS: Mfr. by Niels Vodder
DIMENSIONS: W 27¼" (69.2 cm),
D 30¾" (78.1 cm), H 32¼"
(81.9 cm), SH 14½" (36.8 cm)

Danish architect and designer Finn Juhl was one of the few designers who dominated the European furniture markets during the 1940s and 1950s. He opened his own office in 1945 to design not only furniture, but also glassware, carpets, light fixtures, and refrigerators. This easy chair has a frame of lacquered or oiled teak with a "floating" seat (resting on two edges) and back upholstered in hand-woven wool. It won the Gold Medal at the Milan Triennale in 1951.

PEACOCK CHAIR (JH 550), 1947

DESIGNER: Hans Wegner
STYLE: Danish Modern
COUNTRY: Denmark
STATUS: Mfr. by Johannes Hansens Møbelsnedkeri; Dist. by DSI
DIMENSIONS: W 30¼″ (76.8 cm), D 30½″ (77.5 cm), H 40½″ (102.9 cm), SH 14¼″ (36.2 cm)

Wegner was inspired by tradition in his chair designs—the Chinese Chair was modeled after a Ming Dynasty piece, and this Peacock Chair, also known as JH 550, reworks a traditional Windsor-style chair. The name Peacock comes from a description of the back as being like a fanned peacock's tail. Made of solid ash with teak armrests and a paper cord seat, this design is as dramatic as a peacock's tail display even without color.

CHINA CHAIR, 1946

DESIGNER: Hans Wegner (b. 1914)
STYLE: Danish Modern
COUNTRY: Denmark
STATUS: Mfr. by Fritz Hansen; Dist. by Rudd International
DIMENSIONS: W 21½″ (54.5 cm), D 21½″ (54.5 cm), H 32¼″ (81.9 cm)

Danish wood furniture is world famous. In part this reputation is due to Hans Wegner, the "master of sitting." He opened his office in 1943 in Gentofte, Denmark, where he designed many products besides chairs: wallpaper, silverware, and light fixtures. But he is known worldwide for his lightly scaled chairs. Modeled on a Chinese chair in Copenhagen's Museum of Decorative Art, the frame is made of natural or stained beech or cherrywood. The reversible seat pad is available in black or brown leather.

"THE" CHAIR, 1949

DESIGNER: Hans Wegner
STYLE: Danish Modern
COUNTRY: Denmark
STATUS: Mfr. by Johannes
Hansens Møbelsnedkeri;
Dist. by DSI
DIMENSIONS: W 24¾" (62.9 cm),
D 20½" (52.1 cm), H 30"
(76.2 cm), SH 17" (43 cm)

Wegner trained at the Copenhagen School of Arts and
Crafts and later became a lec-
turer there, from 1946 to

1953. His beautiful wood
chairs are sturdy but not at all
heavy; their lightness makes
them suitable for mass production. This one, also known as
JH 501 or the Classic Chair, is
made of solid oak. The original
had Siamese teak legs and an
oak top rail. (Teak and oak are
his favorite woods.) Now the
frame is made totally of solid
oak and the seat is caned or of
fabric. The wood for this chair
is aged for two years before
being fabricated.

CHAIR 24, 1950

DESIGNER: Hans Wegner
STYLE: Danish Modern
COUNTRY: Denmark
STATUS: Mfr. by Carl Hansen
and Son;
Dist. by DSI
DIMENSIONS: W 22½" (57 cm),
D 20½" (52.1 cm), H 28¼"
(71.8 cm), SH 15¼" (38.7 cm)

The beautifully sculpted
"Wishbone" chair, as it is

sometimes called because of its
prominent "Y" split back, is
made of oil-finished smoked
oak or beech, with a paper
string seat. For a lounge chair
it is lightweight and comfortable; the proportions are perfect with a curved rail and split
back. One of Wegner's popular
designs, Chair 24 is now available in a wide variety of
finishes, including nine lacquer colors.

ANT (SERIES 7) CHAIR 3107, 1955

DESIGNER: Arne Jacobsen
(1902–1971)
COUNTRY: Denmark
STATUS: Mfr. by Fritz Hansen;
Dist. by Rudd International
DIMENSIONS: W 19¾" (50.2 cm),
D 20½" (52.7 cm), H 30¾"
(78.1 cm), SH 17¼" (43.8 cm)

Here is the first Danish chair to be designed for mass production. Arne Jacobsen, the versatile architect who de-signed it, used nine layers of wood—seven of beech, as well as teak and oak or maple—which were steamed and molded and glued together. (Now the seat-back is also available upholstered or lacquered.) The cutouts, which make the chair ant-shaped, increase the flexibility of the back. Rubber dampers connect the seat to satin chrome-plated tubular steel (originally wood) legs. It can be stacked.

SWAN AND EGG, 1958

DESIGNER: Arne Jacobsen
COUNTRY: Denmark
STATUS: Mfr. by Fritz Hansen;
Dist. by Rudd International
DIMENSIONS: Swan: D 26¾"
(67.9 cm), H 29½" (74.9 cm);
Egg: W 34" (86.4 cm), D 31"
(78.7 cm), H 42" (106.7 cm)

Arne Jacobsen, the Danish designer, is one of the few people ever to create a truly new chair idea. This charming pair sent Scandinavian design spinning in a different direction from the wood sculptures of Wegner. Created for the lobby of the SAS Hotel in Copenhagen, Swan and Egg (along with a Swan Sofa) were made of molded fiberglass shells with latex foam padding glued on. The chairs are difficult to produce because the fabric, vinyl, or leather upholstery must fit exactly. The seats swivel on columns of chromed steel over four-legged star-shaped bases of polished cast aluminum.

OXFORD COLLECTION, 1963

DESIGNER: Arne Jacobsen
COUNTRY: Denmark
STATUS: Mfr. by Fritz Hansen;
Dist. by Rudd International
DIMENSIONS: W 25¼" (64.1 cm),
D 21¼" (54 cm), H variable

The Oxford Collection was created for an architecture project of Arne Jacobsen's: St. Catherine's College. The leather or fabric-upholstered chairs have backs of varying heights; some have armrests. The seat heights can be adjusted. Mounted on star-shaped metal bases, some with casters, some of the seats tilt. The collection includes some tables with T-bar or pedestal metal bases.

LAMINATED WOOD CHAIR AND OTTOMAN, 1963

DESIGNER: Grete Jalk
STYLE: Danish Modern
COUNTRY: Denmark
STATUS: Not in production

The sculpted frame of this chair and ottoman is made of molded, laminated Oregon pine with an optional upholstered seat and back. Jalk has modified this theme a number of times—creating stools, tables, and chairs. This chair was formerly produced by P. Jeppesen Company, which was destroyed by fire in the mid-1980s.

ARMCHAIR 11, 1957

DESIGNER: Poul Kjaerholm
COUNTRY: Denmark
STATUS: Mfr. by Fritz Hansen;
Dist. by Rudd International
DIMENSIONS: W 25¼" (64.1 cm),
D 17¾" (45.1 cm), H 25½"
(64.8 cm), SH 16¼" (41.3 cm)

This charming three-legged armchair, winner of the Milan Triennale Grand Prize in 1957, takes up very little space. It has a chrome-plated steel frame—Kjaerholm liked metal frames—with arms made of ash or oak formed in a graceful curve. The seat is made of parchment, oxhide, or canvas.

CHAIR 22, 1956

DESIGNER: Poul Kjaerholm,
(1929–1980)
STYLE: Danish Modern
COUNTRY: Denmark
STATUS: Mfr. by Fritz Hansen;
Dist. by Rudd International
DIMENSIONS: W 24¾" (62.9 cm),
D 24¾" (62.9 cm), H 30" (76.2 cm)

Architect Poul Kjaerholm's work furthers the new direction taken in Arne Jacobsen's Ant Chair (page 102). Kjaerholm used metal rather than wood frames and designed for mass production. Here he used steel rods where earlier designers might have used tubular steel. Kjaerholm preferred natural materials, like most Danish designers, for seats; cane, leather, canvas, parchment, oxhide, slate, wood, and rope were among his choices. This chair has a wicker or leather seat and a chrome-plated flat section steel base.

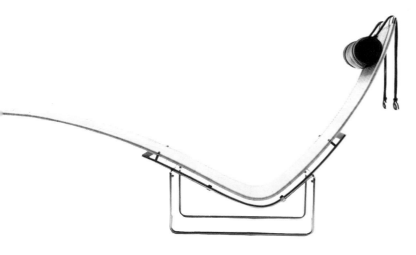

HAMMOCK CHAIR 24, 1966

DESIGNER: Poul Kjaerholm
COUNTRY: Denmark
STATUS: Mfr. by Fritz Hansen;
Dist. by Rudd International
DIMENSIONS: W 26¼" (66.7 cm),
D 61" (154.9 cm), H 34¼"
(87 cm), SH 7¼" (18.4 cm)

Extremely light, the Hammock Chair seems to nearly disappear when looked at from the side. Its stainless steel frame supports a handwoven cane seat and back, and a small tubelike headrest cushion is covered in leather or goatskin. Though similar in concept to Le Corbusier's Pony Chaise (page 71)—its angle can be changed at will, and there is a clear distinction between support and supported elements—this chair is quite a bit lighter.

CHAIR 20, 1968

DESIGNER: Poul Kjaerholm
COUNTRY: Denmark
STATUS: Mfr. by Fritz Hansen;
Dist. by Rudd International
DIMENSIONS: W 31½" (80 cm),
D 26¾" (67.9 cm), H 28¾"
(73 cm), SH 14½" (36.8 cm)

Poul Kjaerholm's Chair 20 is often compared to the Tugendhat Chair of Mies van der Rohe (page 68), and for obvious reasons. The cantilevered steel frame supports a leather seat of oxhide sewn in horizontal strips. But the seat is stretched across the frame, and the frame is prestressed and connected by a transverse steel yoke. Kjaerholm made the scale lighter, and he used a fundamentally different technology. Like other Kjaerholm chairs, the 20 is elegant, balanced, and innovative.

PANTONOVA WIRE FURNITURE, 1961–1966

DESIGNER: Verner Panton
COUNTRY: Denmark/Switzerland
STATUS: Not in production

Born in Denmark, Verner Panton has worked in his own office near Basel, Switzerland since 1963. Educated at Odense Technical School and the Copenhagen Royal Academy of Fine Arts, Panton collaborated with Arne Jacobsen in the 1950s. His wire furniture can be grouped in serpentine or scalloped fashion to any desired length. This collection was formerly manufactured by Fritz Hansen and Panton Design.

STACKING CHAIR, 1960–1968

DESIGNER: Verner Panton (b. 1926)
COUNTRY: Denmark/Switzerland
STATUS: Mfr. by Horn GmbH;
Dist. by Nienkämper
DIMENSIONS: W 19" (48.3 cm),
D 21½" (54.5 cm), H 33¼"
(84.5 cm), SH 17" (42.8 cm)

The Panton Stacking Chair is the first example of a single-form molded fiberglass chair, now made of polyurethane. The cantilevered seat has Art Nouveau curves, but it is often compared to the Zigzag Chair by Rietveld (page 58). Indeed, Rietveld had tried to create a single-form chair and failed, but of course he had no fiberglass molding technology in 1934. This chair is strong, durable, comfortable, and appealing. Included in the Permanent Collection of The Museum of Modern Art in New York City, this stacking chair is a thoroughly modern idea. It comes in several colors.

PANTON SYSTEM 1-2-3, 1974

DESIGNER: Verner Panton
COUNTRY: Denmark/Switzerland
STATUS: Mfr. by Fritz Hansen;
Dist. by Rud.
Rasmussens Snedkerier
DIMENSIONS: Variable

This system consists of a series of chairs and easy chairs with three different seat heights. Available with or without armrests, these chairs, with their gracefully flowing backs and a variety of bases, have two types of padding. They interlock in a unique way to form a sophisticated seating unit for a variety of settings. Many upholstery fabrics are available.

CHAIR 290/ ARMCHAIR 291, 1965

DESIGNER: Steen Ostergaard
COUNTRY: Denmark
STATUS: Not in production

Chair 290 is a stackable cantilever chair made of nylon and reinforced with fiberglass. It is lightweight and strong but looks very delicate. Available in a silky gloss finish in white, brown, red, beige, or blue, the chair resists static electricity as well as weather. These chairs were formerly manufactured by Cado.

ASSERBO CHAIR 504, 1964

DESIGNER: Børge Mogensen (b. 1914)
COUNTRY: Denmark
STATUS: Mfr. by AB Karl Andersson & söner
DIMENSIONS: W 24¾" (62.9 cm), D 19¾" (50.2 cm), H 29½" (74.9 cm), SH 17" (42.8 cm)

Børge Mogensen was trained by Kaare Klint. When he became the head of the furniture factory owned by the Danish Consumers' Cooperative (FDB Mobler), he had an opportunity to develop his functional, crafted furniture. He felt that "furniture should become more beautiful with use, like well-worn sports equipment." Asserbo Chair 504 comes with or without arms in clear or colored lacquer finishes. The outer edge of the Swedish pine frame is rounded for comfort. The sea grass seat is plaited on a removable frame.

MUSHROOM CHAIR, 1965

DESIGNER: Eero Aarnio (b. 1932)
COUNTRY: Finland
STATUS: Mfr. by Asko
DIMENSIONS: W 33″ (83.8 cm),
D 35″ (88.9 cm), H 26″ (66 cm),
SH 14½″ (36.8 cm)

Eero Aarnio, the Finnish industrial and interior designer, created the Mushroom Chair in 1965, two years after opening his own office near Helsinki. Preoccupied with rounded forms, Aarnio has designed furniture of fiberglass as well as wicker and rattan; he has won many prizes and honors for his industrial designs. This popular and much-copied chair and ottoman are made by hand of bleached rattan.

GLOBE, BALL, BOMB, OR SPHERE, 1966

DESIGNER: Eero Aarnio
COUNTRY: Finland
STATUS: Mfr. by Asko
DIMENSIONS: H 47½″ (120.5 cm),
W 41¼″ (104.8 cm), D 38½″
(97.8 cm), SH 18″ (45.7 cm)

Aarnio was instrumental in the development of molded fiberglass shell furniture. He had a one-man show of his designs in this medium in 1968 in Stockholm and Helsinki. This chair was commissioned by its manufacturer as a publicity stunt. A dramatic and innovative shape, it has been used repeatedly in movies and television to symbolize the "mod" style of the 1960s. The shell is white, and the interior—upholstered with polyester over Dacron and foam—comes in a variety of colors. Some knock-offs inspired by Globe have stereo speakers built in; others have lighting systems and bars.

GYRO, PASTILLI, OR ROCK 'N' ROLL CHAIR, 1968

DESIGNER: Eero Aarnio
COUNTRY: Finland
STATUS: Mfr. by Asko
DIMENSIONS: W 35½″ (90.1 cm),
D 35½″ (90.1 cm), H 20½″
(52.1 cm), SH 8″ (20.3 cm)

After designing the Globe and Mushroom, Aarnio designed this novel candy-shaped seat and won the AID (now ASID—for American Society of Interior Designers) Award in 1968. The Gyro (or Pastilli, or Rock 'N' Roll) is offered in a variety of colors. It is made of molded fiberglass, with a seam encircling the form like an equator. It can be used outdoors—even at the beach or in the snow—and is very popular with both children and adults.

CHAIR 9230, 1967

DESIGNER: Henning Larsen (b. 1925)
COUNTRY: Denmark
STATUS: Mfr. by Fritz Hansen
Dist. by Rudd International
DIMENSIONS: W 20½″ (52.1 cm),
D 17″ (42.8 cm), H 26″ (66 cm),
SH 17½″ (44.6 cm)

After training in Copenhagen, London, and Boston, Henning Larsen worked with Arne Jacobsen and, later, with Jørn Utzon. Since 1968 he has been a professor of architecture at the Royal Academy in Copenhagen. He opened his own office in 1969. A drop-leaf wood table with steel legs was also designed to complement this bent tubular steel chair in 1967.

KARUSELLI, 1965

DESIGNER: Yrjö Kukkapuro
(b. 1933)
COUNTRY: Finland
STATUS: Mfr. by Avarte
DIMENSIONS: W 31″ (78.7 cm),
D 37¾″ (95.9 cm), H 36″ (91.4 cm)

Yrjö Kukkapuro's Karuselli Chair rocks and swivels on a chrome-plated steel cradle. Its base is a star shape. Its seat is a steel-reinforced fiberglass shell with leather upholstery. Kukkapuro, who is an architect and a designer, specializes in innovative uses of new materials—working like an engineer to exploit them for his designs. During the 1980s he became associated with the Italian Memphis group.

FLOATING DOCK, 1967

DESIGNER: Jørn Utzon (b. 1918)
COUNTRY: Denmark
STATUS: Mfr. by Fritz Hansen
DIMENSIONS: H 22¾" (57.8 cm),
D 48¾" (123.8 cm), W 29"
(73.7 cm), SH 9½" (24.1 cm)

Jørn Utzon, one of Denmark's leading architects, urban planners, and industrial designers, received international recognition for his spectacular opera house in Sydney, Australia.

Utzon's furniture is a notable departure from the Teak Style, popular in Denmark during the previous decades. The Floating Dock, recipient of many design awards, has an extended aluminum frame filled with molded foam rubber cushions. Floating Dock is part of a series that includes a variety of different furniture pieces, and is based on a system of component arcs that lock at 45-degree angles.

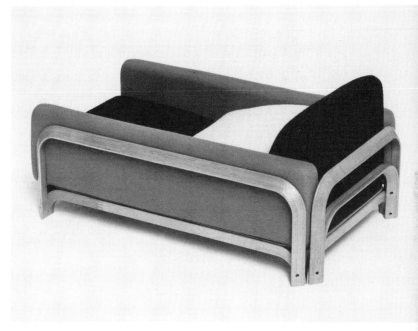

ROYAL FURNITURE, 1969

DESIGNER: Rud Thygesen
and Johnny Sorensen
COUNTRY: Denmark
STATUS: Mfr. by Botium
DIMENSIONS: W 30" (76.2 cm),
D 82¼" (158 cm), H 30"
(76.2 cm), SH 13½" (34.3 cm)

Thygesen and Sorensen won the 1978 Furniture Prize in Denmark for overall excellence, along with Verner Panton. This furniture was designed for a Cabinetmakers' Guild of Copenhagen competition in 1969. It won first prize and was presented to King Frederik IX for his 70th birthday. The range of tables and chairs have frames of solid oak, beech, or Honduran mahogany. Seats and backs are made of French caning. The chaise was recently selected for the permanent collection of the Victoria and Albert Museum, London.

POSTWAR AMERICA

In both originality and timing, the United States lagged behind Europe in the design of modern furniture. From the crafts period—with the significant exception of the Prairie School—not much new design ground was broken. American designers worked in European idioms, and even through the 1940s the great styles came primarily from Europe. Imports dominated the contract market—furniture from Denmark and Finland, from Germany, France, and Austria.

And then came Charles Eames. With his wife Ray, Eames began to work in a uniquely American style while building on the technological developments of the Scandinavians. Eames invented a technique for bending plywood into complex curves—taking the work done by Aalto a step further—while making leg splints in the United States Navy during World War II. Eames and his Cranbrook Academy colleague, Eero Saarinen, energized American design and sent it forward into new looks, new materials.

The chief designer of Herman Miller—which produces Eames's work—was George Nelson. He also had new ideas to contribute—taking the Klint sideboard idea, for example, and coming up with a new American furniture favorite, the wall unit. (This was also being done in Germany in the 1950s by Hans Gugelot and Jürgen Lange.) Nelson developed a chair and sofa that introduced a light note into modern

furnishings: Coconut and Marshmallow, as they were called, dictated the shape of the 1950s and predicted the 1980s to come as well. They were a far cry (for some a welcome change) from the seriousness of earlier modern works.

Besides Herman Miller, the important furniture company in the postwar United States has been Knoll International—which was founded by two Cranbrook affiliates, Florence and Hans Knoll, in the middle 1950s. They produced the work not only of Americans but also of Bauhaus designers, putting many classics of the 1920s back into mass production.

New York City's Museum of Modern Art, founded in the 1930s, was an important influence in the development of good design in the United States after the war. By sponsoring shows and competitions for innovative furniture designs, the museum stimulated many talented people and attracted worldwide attention.

Market demand for more contract design also stimulated fresh solutions for more flexible, efficient, convenient furnishings for offices. In the 1960s systems furniture became popular: components could be combined to suit the space and taste of the consumer. While the idea was not altogether new—Verner Panton, for example, created his wire system furniture with variable combinations in mind—Americans brought the idea to fruition.

EAMES® LCM DINING CHAIR, 1946

DESIGNERS: Charles (1907–1978) and Ray Kaiser Eames
COUNTRY: United States
STATUS: Mfr. by Herman Miller
DIMENSIONS: W 22¼" (56.5 cm), D 25⅜" (64.4 cm), H 27⅜" (69.6 cm), 29½" (74.9 cm), SH 15¼" (38.7 cm)

Charles Eames and his wife Ray experimented with molded plywood for chairs while they were both at the Cranbrook Academy. Originally made in two heights—for lounging or dining—of ash, birch, or walnut (only walnut veneer is available now), the seat and back were attached to the frame of chrome-plated steel rods with rubber shock mounts. The complex curve of the wood and the rubber mounts made upholstery unnecessary. Eames protected the tips of the legs with rubber caps (now plastic glides). This chair is one of Eames's most popular and most beautiful designs.

EAMES® DCW MOLDED PLYWOOD CHAIR, 1946

DESIGNERS: Charles and Ray Eames
COUNTRY: United States
STATUS: Not in production

Soon after sharing the first prize in The Museum of Modern Art's Organic Design in Home Furnishings competition with Eero Saarinen, Eames focused on the organic and sculptural potential of molded plywood. This chair is made of molded walnut plywood on a frame of bent walnut plywood. The seat and back are mounted on rubber like the seat of the LCM (page 114). Later the chair was made of birch. George Nelson, who was the first design director of Herman Miller, was instrumental in bringing Eames's work to Herman Miller. Eames's earliest chairs were made by Evans Products Company and the Eames® DCW Molded Plywood Chair was produced by it from 1946 to 1953.

EAMES® DAR SHELL CHAIR, 1950

DESIGNERS: Charles and Ray Eames
COUNTRY: United States
STATUS: Mfr. by Herman Miller
DIMENSIONS: W 24⅞" (63.2 cm),
D 24" (61 cm), H 31½" (80 cm),
SH 17⅞" (45.4 cm)

The DAR was the first mass-produced molded fiberglass shell chair (although the design was at first executed in stamped metal). What a change this made in furniture. One problem for a while had been the difficulty of attaching legs to the shell. The Eameses solved this problem with rubber connectors, and the chair could be mass-produced easily. They made many versions of this model through the years, and the chair is now available in a number of finishes and sculptural forms. A group of DAR chairs won second prize in The Museum of Modern Art's International Competition for Low-Cost Furniture Design in 1948.

EAMES® DKR SHELL CHAIR, 1951

DESIGNERS: Charles and Ray Eames
COUNTRY: United States
STATUS: Not in production

Charles and Ray Eames did not stay at Cranbrook. They moved to Santa Monica, California, where they designed their own home, called the Case Study House. This house, plus their innovative chair designs, has made them America's preeminent designers of the period, and changed the look of design forever. This DKR dining or desk chair (also known as the "Bikini") has a black wire base with self-leveling floor glides and a black or white wire frame. The upholstery is a one-piece pad and comes in several colors. It was formerly produced by Herman Miller from 1952 to 1966.

EAMES® LOUNGE CHAIR 670, 1956

DESIGNERS: Charles and Ray Eames
COUNTRY: United States
STATUS: Mfr. by Herman Miller
DIMENSIONS: W 32½″ (82.6 cm),
D 32¾″ (83.1 cm), H 33⅜″
(84.8 cm), SH 15″ (38.1 cm)

The Eames Chair, as this lounge is widely known, is the twentieth century's answer to the old wing or club chair. Made for comfort and luxury, it won the hearts of many who resisted innovation. The Eameses used a five-ply molded wood shell with rosewood veneer made in a hot-press metal die upholstered in leather or fabric and mounted on a five-prong pedestal base. The arms are made of 12-gauge steel plates bonded with foam pads and upholstered. The separate wood forms of the back are joined with aluminum and rubber shock mounts, allowing maximum flexibility. In the edges of the wood shells, the layers are visible; the outside of the shells is hand-rubbed with wax.

EAMES® ALUMINUM GROUP CHAIR, 1958

DESIGNERS: Charles and Ray Eames
COUNTRY: United States
STATUS: Mfr. by Herman Miller
DIMENSIONS: W 24¾″ (62.9 cm),
D 28½″ (72.4 cm), H 33¼″
(84.5 cm), SH 17½″ (44.6 cm)

This versatile Aluminum Group consists of six metal components in two styles in a wide range of sizes, chairs with or without arms. Here a black steel stem on the pedestal base supports a bonelike aluminum frame which holds the seat. It has no internal metal. Instead, a fabric sandwich construction was used. An inner layer of vinyl-coated nylon fabric was fused with foam, upholstered in leather or Naugahyde or fabric, and welded horizontally to make stripes. Two later versions had foam filled leather cushions.

EAMES® TANDEM SLING SEATING, 1962

DESIGNERS: Charles and Ray Eames
COUNTRY: United States
STATUS: Mfr. by Herman Miller
DIMENSIONS: Variable

This seating system can be seen in many public waiting areas. Seat and back cushions are slings, supported only at the sides. The base is made of black epoxy finished steel T-beams with steel connector bars. Seats have interchangeable black vinyl-upholstered foam pads, the armrests are padded and covered to match, and the base has plastic glides. The overall widths of the assembled units are the same as the base widths. It is sturdy despite its delicate design.

EAMES® CHAISE, 1968

DESIGNERS: Charles and Ray Eames
COUNTRY: United States
STATUS: Mfr. by Herman Miller
DIMENSIONS: L 75" (190.5 cm),
D 17½" (44.6 cm), H 28¾"
(73 cm), SH 20½" (52.1 cm)

This handsome lounge was another answer to those who felt that luxury and comfort must be sacrificed for innovation. Its bonelike legs recall the aluminum structure of the Aluminum Group (page 116); the frame and base have an eggplant stretched and plasticized nylon coating, and the cushions are attached to each other by zippers. They are padded with polyester foam and upholstered in black leather.

WOMB CHAIR, 1946

DESIGNER: Eero Saarinen
(1910–1961)
COUNTRY: United States
STATUS: Mfr. by Knoll International
DIMENSIONS: Chair: W 40"
(101.6 cm), D 34" (86.4 cm),
H 35½" (90.1 cm),
SH 16" (40.6 cm);
Ottoman: W 25½" (64.8 cm), D 20"
(50.8 cm), H 16" (40.6 cm)

A great American architect and furniture designer, and the son of Eliel Saarinen, Eero Saarinen became famous for the General Motors Technical Center in Warren, Michigan, the TWA Terminal at Kennedy Airport in New York, and the Dulles Airport in Virginia. Named by Saarinen for the security it gives to the sitter, the Womb Chair combines a maximum of comfort and a minimum of bulk, constructed of a foam molded plastic shell with fabric covered latex foam upholstery. The frame is a bent steel rod base with a polished chrome finish. It has two separate cushions.

TULIP PEDESTAL GROUP, 1957

DESIGNER: Eero Saarinen
COUNTRY: United States
STATUS: Mfr. by Knoll International
DIMENSIONS: Chair: W 19½"
(49.5 cm), D 22" (55.9 cm),
H 32½" (82.6 cm),
SH 18½" (47 cm);
Armchair: W 26" (66 cm), D 23½"
(59.7 cm), H 32" (81.2 cm),
SH 18½" (47 cm)

Saarinen joined his friends the Knolls at Knoll International in 1943. Soon he was making models of one-leg designs that were to revolutionize the furniture industry. His goal was to clear up the "slum of legs" under the table. The chairs were made in three parts: a plastic-coated cast aluminum base, a molded plastic shell reinforced with fiberglass, and a latex foam pad, covered with upholstery held on by zippers (now Velcro). The form is organically unified. Tulip is available now in two colors, gray-beige and white.

IN50 TABLE, 1944

DESIGNER: Isamu Noguchi (b. 1904)
COUNTRY: United States/Japan
STATUS: Mfr. by Herman Miller
DIMENSIONS: W 50"
(127 cm), D 36" (91.4 cm),
H 15¾" (40 cm)

Isamu Noguchi, the renowned sculptor, has designed only a few pieces of furniture. This table is made of a walnut or ebony-finished poplar base in two parts topped by a plate glass rounded triangle. The wood pieces are sculpture, visible through the top, arranged in an intriguing top to bottom fashion. It was produced by Herman Miller from 1947 through 1972, and then from 1984 on.

HIGHBACK LOUNGE CHAIR, 1951

DESIGNER: Harry Bertoia
(1915–1978)
COUNTRY: United States
STATUS: Mfr. by Knoll International
DIMENSIONS: W 38½" (97.8 cm),
D 34½" (87.8 cm), H 39" (99.1 cm)

Harry Bertoia was trained at the Cranbrook Academy when Florence and Hans Knoll, founders of Knoll International, were there. They employed Bertoia to do what he felt like, as they put it, and he developed a series of chairs using welded steel rods. These three are all constructed of chrome-plated or plastic-coated steel rod frames and a welded lattice wire shell. The seat of the armchair is suspended for greater flexibility. Pads are available for all models, but the chairs are made (by hand) mostly of air. Bertoia believed that "chairs are studies in space, form, and metal too."

T-CHAIR, 1952

DESIGNERS: William Katavolos (b. 1924); Ross Littell (b. 1924); Douglas Kelly (b. 1924)
COUNTRY: United States
STATUS: Mfr. by ICF, Italy
DIMENSIONS: H 24½″ (69.2 cm)

The T-Chair was the product of a successful collaboration between these three designers. Because of its unity of form— all components are based on the T shape—it won the AID design award in 1952 and was included in The Museum of Modern Art's Good Design shows in 1953 and 1955. Four Ts of chrome-plated or black enamelled steel make up the frame; a leather sling curves over the back and side supports like scrolls. The chair is comfortable and stable.

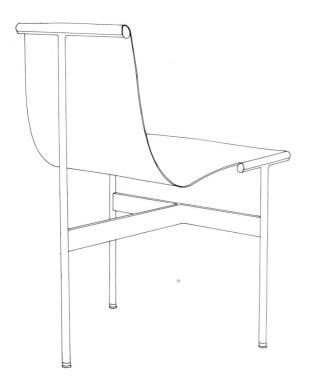

KANTAN COLLECTION, 1956

DESIGNER: Tadao E. Inouye (1917–1980)
COUNTRY: United States
STATUS: Not in production

Introduced in 1956, Kantan's distinctive look was quickly recognized by the industrial and interior design professionals. It won the design award of the Pasadena Art Museum in 1958, and in May, 1959, it was chosen to be a part of the United States Exhibit at the World's Fair held in Tokyo. Alcoa Aluminum used Kantan to illustrate outstanding design incorporating tubular aluminum in 1960. In 1968, it was chosen to be a part of the prestigious Please Be Seated show cosponsored by the American Federation of Arts and the Cooper-Hewitt Museum in New York City. It was formerly manufactured by Brown Jordan.

GEORGE NELSON ARMCHAIR, 1952

DESIGNER: John Pile
COUNTRY: United States
STATUS: Not in production

This chair (*left*), a descendent of the Thonet B-9 Chair (page 13), was originally designed by John Pile for George Nelson and was sold by Herman Miller. It was later recreated by Norman Cherner in 1958 (*center*), and then again by Paul Goldman, the founder of Plycraft. Goldman's version, the Rockwell Chair (*right*), differs greatly from the early one. It is currently manufactured by Plycraft. The Cherner version is available from 50/Fifty.

NELSON COCONUT CHAIR, 1956

DESIGNER: George Nelson
(1908–1986)
COUNTRY: United States
STATUS: Not in production

George Nelson became the first director of design at Herman Miller in 1946. He designed this chair, inspired by the shape of a cracked coconut, in 1956. It has a low brake-formed welded sheet-steel shell mounted on a steel rod base. The shell is padded and upholstered. Produced from 1956 until 1978, it has again become a popular collectible.

NELSON MARSHMALLOW SOFA, 1956

DESIGNER: George Nelson
COUNTRY: United States
STATUS: Not in production

The Marshmallow Sofa, designed by George Nelson with Irving Harper, illustrates the whimsical style of the 1950s in the United States. The avant-garde Memphis design group (see pages 182–183) helped to make the style appealing once again in the 1980s. This sofa was made of leather or Naugahyde covered foam disks attached with foam-plated connectors to a supporting steel frame. Only a few hundred were produced, by Herman Miller, between 1956 and 1965. It came in various shocking color combinations—orange, pink, and purple.

NELSON COMPREHENSIVE STORAGE SYSTEM, 1959

DESIGNER: George Nelson
COUNTRY: United States
STATUS: Not in production

George Nelson made a tremendous contribution to American homes when he designed his first wall system, in 1945, for a feature in *Life* magazine. He refined the design several times, and in 1959 Herman Miller began to produce this Comprehensive Storage System. Components of the system could be rearranged to suit the needs of the owner. There were shelves, cupboards, and work surfaces to choose from, all suspended from aluminum poles. CSS was produced until 1973. Nelson also designed an L-shaped desk that Herman Miller produced as part of its Executive Office Group from 1950 to 1978.

NELSON SLING SOFA, 1964

DESIGNER: George Nelson
COUNTRY: United States
STATUS: Mfr. by Herman Miller
DIMENSIONS: W 87" (221 cm), D 32¼" (81.9 cm), H 29¾" (75.6 cm), SH 15½" (39.4 cm)

One of America's leading furniture designers, George Nelson was also a graphic artist, author, and architect. He planned several influential exhibitions as well, including the American Exhibition in Moscow in 1959. His Sling Sofa has a raised frame of polished chromed-steel tubing—the sections are joined by epoxy resin. Leather upholstered cushions are filled with urethane foam within polyester fiber batting. They are supported by fabric reinforced rubber straps at the back and neoprene sheets across the seat.

WILLOW (W-5) CHAIR, 1962

DESIGNER: Elinor McGuire
COUNTRY: United States
STATUS: Mfr. by The McGuire Company
DIMENSIONS: W 44″ (111.8 cm), D 32″ (81.2), H 42″ (106.7 cm), Frame SH: 15″ (38.1 cm)

Elinor and John McGuire and a few others have created hundreds of elegant rattan and wicker furnishings. The Willow Chair has emerged as a classic. Loose cushions and back upholstery are available in a wide range of colors and patterns.

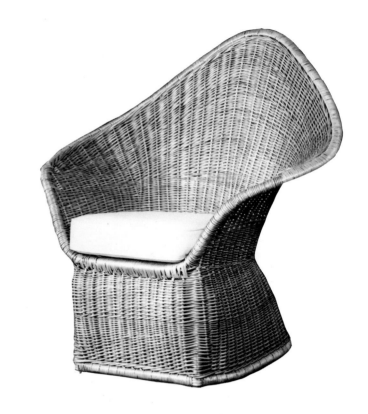

RATTAN OH-9 OFFICER'S CHAIR, 1952

DESIGNER: Eleanor Forbes
COUNTRY: United States
STATUS: Mfr. by The McGuire Company
DIMENSIONS: W 24″ (61 cm), D 23″ (58.4 cm), H 31″ (78.7 cm), AH 23″ (58.4 cm), SH 15″ (38.1 cm)

John and Elinor McGuire established their company in 1948 in San Francisco. Through the years, the hallmark of this company has been rattan (a solid jungle vine from the Orient) and rawhide furniture. In 1952, the McGuires commissioned Eleanor Forbes, who was then working as an interior designer for Gump's of San Francisco, to create a rattan chair that was both beautiful and light—very different from the heavy, ugly rattan pieces available at that time. This officer's chair and ottoman are both now part of The Museum of Modern Art's Permanent Collection.

ACTION OFFICE® SYSTEM, 1964

DESIGNER: Robert L. Propst
(b. 1921)
COUNTRY: United States
STATUS: Mfr. by Herman Miller
DIMENSIONS: Variable, depending
on components chosen

Action Office® was the idea of Robert Propst, who became head of Herman Miller's Research Division in 1960. Propst designed a system of components that could be ar-ranged and rearranged into office settings. Vertical panels of wood and plastic with polished aluminum legs support work surfaces, drawers, shelves, lights, and more. Footrests are chrome plated; writing surfaces are vinyl. Levels and placement of components are up to the user. The Action Office® System is extremely popular; more than two billion dollars worth was sold between 1968 and 1984.

GF 40/4 CHAIR, 1964

DESIGNER: David Rowland (b. 1924)
COUNTRY: United States
STATUS: Mfr. by GF
Furniture Systems
DIMENSIONS: W 20" (50.8 cm),
D 21½" (54.5 cm), H 30"
(76.2 cm), SH 15½" (39.4 cm)

Industrial designer David Rowland trained at the Cranbrook Academy of Art and then opened his own office in 1955. He worked on this stacking chair for eight years. Its frame is constructed of chrome-plated steel rods ⁷⁄₁₆" in diameter; its seat and back are vinyl-covered sheet metal (in six colors) or five-ply wood laminate. Forty of these rigid chairs can be stacked only four feet high on a special trolley. This chair won the Grand Prize at the 1964 Milan Triennale and the AID International Design Award in 1965. It is used in the library of The Museum of Modern Art in New York City.

PLATNER WIRE COLLECTION, 1964–1966

DESIGNER: Warren Platner (b. 1919)
COUNTRY: United States
STATUS: Mfr. by Knoll International
DIMENSIONS: Easy Chair: W 40¾″
(103.5 cm), D 36½″ (92.7 cm),
H 30½″ (77.5 cm);
Lounge: W 36½″ (92.7 cm),
D 25½″ (64.8 cm),
H 30½″ (77.5 cm);
Armchair: W 26½″ (67.3 cm),
D 22″ (55.9 cm), H 29″ (73.7 cm)

Warren Platner, an architect as well as a furniture and interior designer, graduated from Cornell University. He opened his own firm in 1967. He collaborated with the Knoll International Design Development Group on wire furniture from 1965 until 1967. The collection includes a large lounge, an armchair, an easy chair, an ottoman, a stool, and several tables. The wire base common to all these pieces is unique. It is made of electrically welded steel rods with a bright nickel finish. Lounge and easy chairs have foam cushions for seat and back over a molded fiberglass shell. Tabletops are glass, marble, or wood.

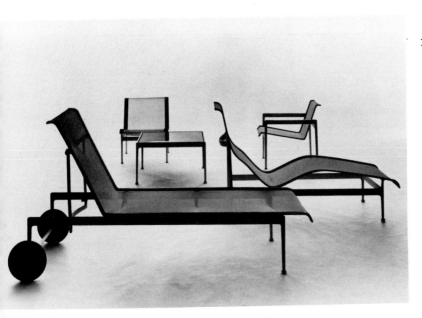

LEISURE COLLECTION, 1966

DESIGNER: Richard Schultz
(b. 1926)
COUNTRY: United States
STATUS: Mfr. by Knoll International
DIMENSIONS: Lounge: W 23″
(58.4 cm), D 28½″ (72.4 cm),
H 26½″ (67.3 cm);
Chaise: W 25½″ (64.8 cm), L 76″
(193 cm), H 14½–35½″
(36.8–90.1 cm)

Richard Schultz was trained at the Illinois Institute of Technology. In 1951 he joined Knoll International in East Grenville, Pennsylvania. His Leisure Collection, one of the most popular modern outdoor furniture groups ever, includes a chaise lounge, a cart lounge, tables and chairs with or without arms. The frames are made of cast aluminum with a textured weatherproof finish. Seating units are made of Dacron mesh in white or beige stitched to dark brown vinyl strips. The collection won the AID Award in 1967.

SWIVEL ARMCHAIR, 1965

DESIGNER: Charles Pollock (b. 1930)
COUNTRY: United States
STATUS: Mfr. by Knoll International
DIMENSIONS: W 26¼" (66.7 cm),
D 28¼" (71.8 cm), H 31"
(78.7 cm)

Charles Pollock studied at the Pratt Institute in Brooklyn, New York. He worked as an industrial designer for George

Nelson from 1955 to 1959. Later he developed this group of office chairs. Made of molded plastic and polished aluminum, with leather upholstery, these chairs have no inner metal spine and do not fade, rust, or tarnish. Swivel was chosen by *Interior Design* magazine (April 1982) as one of the most significant chairs of the past 50 years.

TUBO TABLE, 1968; CHAIR 424, 1969

DESIGNER: John Mascheroni
(b. 1932)
COUNTRY: United States
STATUS: Mfr. by Mascheroni Designs
DIMENSIONS: Chair: W 32"
(81.2 cm), D 32" (81.2 cm),
H 32" (81.2 cm)

Mascheroni was trained at the Pratt Institute in Brooklyn, New York. His Chair 424 and

the Tubo Table both have frames of tubular polished aluminum sections three inches in diameter. The chair has a wood frame seat covered in multidensity urethane foam and upholstered. A sling of fabric loops up over the armrest support. The table was selected by *Interior Design* as one of the 50 most influential pieces of the modern period.

POSTWAR ITALY

After World War II, Scandinavia humanized the International Style with wood and with careful attention to the needs of consumers. They were not the only inheritors of that austere modern idiom, however. The Italians were also deeply influenced by this period—taking geometry and spareness and machinelike precision for themselves as they developed their own unique approach. The result was the sleek modern Italian style dramatized by The Museum of Modern Art's show in 1972: Italy: The New Domestic Landscape. It was derived from Le Corbusier and Gropius and Breuer, but it employed new materials—plastics, fiberglass, foam—and eliminated structural parts made unnecessary by new technology: springs, webbing, elaborate internal supports. As these cheap new materials were used, and sophisticated but inexpensive machine methods (like injection molding and hot pressing) were also used, good

design became available to nearly everyone.

There was one other important trend in Italian design, new for the modern movement: the trend towards humor. One fault many saw in the International Style was its seriousness—purity bordering on pomposity. Italians like Gilardi, Mollino, Albini, and others in the Design Studio approached furniture design not only with beauty and proportion and comfort in mind, but also with a sense of wit and parody.

Italian design was bolstered and publicized worldwide by several magazines including Giò Ponti's *Domus*, *Casa Vogue*, and *Rassegna*. The competitions also helped: every third year the Milan Triennale, and yearly the Salone del Mobile Italiano. But the main reason Italian design after World War II was considered extremely important was obvious. The Italians led the way into the future with a tremendous sense of style.

SUPERLEGGERA CHAIR 699, 1957

DESIGNER: Giò Ponti (1891–1979)
COUNTRY: Italy
STYLE: Italian Modern
STATUS: Mfr. by Cassina
DIMENSIONS: W 15¾" (40 cm), D 17¼" (43.8 cm), H 32½" (82.6 cm), SH 17¼" (43.8 cm)

Foremost pioneer Italian designer, architect, and painter, Giò Ponti created the magazine *Domus* in 1928. Through the years he designed flatware, ceramic tile, car bodies, toilets, lamps, sewing machines, textiles, and, of course, furniture. This lightly scaled chair is based on a traditional design produced in Chiavari, Italy. The frame is made of ash, walnut, or rosewood, or wood lacquered black or white. The seat is made of plaited cellophane or rubber covered with fabric, vinyl, or leather. In its simplicity it evokes the Shaker style (page 13). Though lightweight, it is durable and sturdy.

FIORENZA CHAIR, 1952

DESIGNER: Franco Albini (b. 1905)
COUNTRY: Italy
STYLE: Milan School
STATUS: Mfr. by Arflex
DIMENSIONS: W 28¾" (73 cm), D 36¼" (92.1 cm), H 40½" (103 cm)

The Milan Triennale competition, begun in 1923 and held every third year, helped to make Milan an important design center after World War II. These neoorganic upholstered reclining and easy chairs by Mollino and Albini express a typical style of the Milan School. Exaggerated shapes are sensuous and sculptural, and dark wood legs balance upholstery by their dramatic presence. Both designers are architects as well as furniture designers.

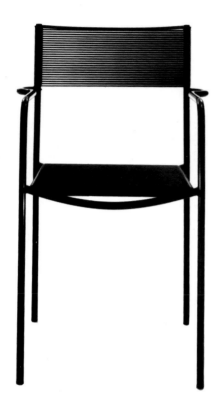

ARMCHAIR 892, circa 1960

DESIGNER: Vico Magistretti (b. 1920)
COUNTRY: Italy
STATUS: Not in production

Architect, urban planner, and furniture designer Vico Magistretti joined his father's firm in 1945 in Milan. His chairs won many awards at the Milan Triennale. This chair is made of beechwood with walnut or natural stains, and is also available in a black or white or red high-gloss finish. The woven grass, cane, or leather seat makes a nice contrast in texture to the wood. This chair was formerly manufactured by Cassina and distributed by Atelier International.

SPAGHETTI CHAIR, 1960

DESIGNER: Giandomenico Belotti (b. 1932)
COUNTRY: Italy
STATUS: Mfr. by ICF
DIMENSIONS: W 21" (53.3 cm), D 20" (50.8 cm), H 32½" (82.6 cm), SH 18" (45.7 cm), AH 26½" (67.3 cm)

Giandomenico Belotti studied sculpture and became an architect. He also designed furniture. This chair was originally called Odessa. It is innovative in combining tubular steel with polyvinyl-chloride "spaghetti" string in excellent proportions. It comes in red, black, and white.

SELENE STACKING CHAIR, 1961

DESIGNER: Vico Magistretti
COUNTRY: Italy
STATUS: Mfr. by Artemide
DIMENSIONS: W 15½" (39.4 cm),
D 19¾" (50.2 cm), H 30" (76.2 cm)

Selene is a molded fiberglass form reinforced with polyester and produced by hot pressing—a process invented by Italian designers. Designed in 1961, it has been produced since 1966. Now available in four colors (at first it was made only in apple green), it was exhibited in Italy: The New Domestic Landscape at The Museum of Modern Art, New York, in 1972. The seat and front leg supports are indented from the back seat and rear leg supports. Selene can be easily stacked.

MEZZADRO TRACTOR SEAT, 1955

DESIGNERS: Achille (b. 1918) and Pier Giacomo Castiglioni
COUNTRY: Italy
STATUS: Mfr. by ICF
DIMENSIONS: W 19¼" (48.9 cm),
D 19¾" (50.2 cm), H 20" (50.8 cm)

The Castiglioni brothers created this chair from a 1935 tractor seat, a bicycle wingnut, a leaf spring from an Italian railways sleeping car, and a beech spindle. The seat comes in green, red, navy, orange, black, yellow, or white lacquer, or in chrome-plated steel. The footrest is made of beech. Rows of Tractor Seats side by side make attractive seating.

ELDA 1005 CHAIR, 1965

DESIGNER: Joe Colombo (1930–1971)
COUNTRY: Italy
STATUS: Mfr. by Comfort, Giorgetti Fratelli & Company
DIMENSIONS: W 37½" (95.3 cm), D 36" (91.4 cm), H 37¾" (95.9 cm), SH 15" (38.1 cm)

Elda instantly became a classic of the 1960s. Made of a broad sculptured plastic frame resting on a tapered drumlike swivel base, it is generously scaled. Its upholstery, in leather, recalls a folded sausage. Joe Colombo, an artist and architect from Milan, perfected the use of plastic. He opened his own office in 1962, and in 1966 he had a one-man show at Design Research in New York. *Interiors* magazine called him a "scientific designer." He won three prizes at Milan Triennales, and Elda won the AID award in 1968.

SMALL CHILD'S CHAIR, 1961

DESIGNERS: Marco Zanuso (b. 1916);
Richard Sapper (b. 1932)
COUNTRY: Italy
STATUS: Mfr. by Kartell
DIMENSIONS: W 10¼" (26.0 cm), D 10½" (26.7 cm), H 19½" (49.5 cm)

The use of polyethylene injection molding to make furniture was pioneered and developed primarily by Italian designers. This low-pressure polyethylene chair is made of pressure-fitted elements: seat, legs, and grid. Designed for kindergartners and first graders, it can also be stacked.

SUZANNE LOUNGE CHAIR, 1965

DESIGNER: Kazuhide Takahama (b. 1930)
COUNTRY: Italy
STATUS: Mfr. by Knoll International
DIMENSIONS: W 30″ (76.2 cm),
D 34⅝″ (86.5 cm),
H 26¾″ (67.9 cm)

The Suzanne Lounge is a simple and inventive idea. The frame is made of tubular steel with a polished chrome finish. Two separate, very plump upholstered polyfoam cushions form the seat and back by attaching to the frame base. The Suzanne Lounge is also available in widths of 60″ (152.4 cm) and 99″ (251.5 cm). It was designed by Kazuhide Takahama, who was born in Japan and has lived in Bologna, Italy, since 1963.

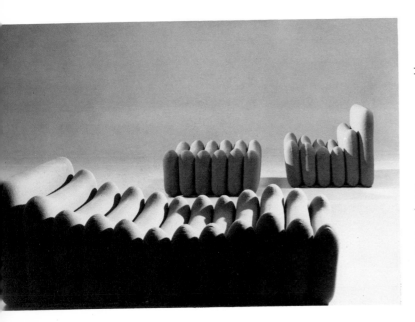

ADDITIONAL SYSTEM LOUNGE, 1968

DESIGNER: Joe Colombo
COUNTRY: Italy
STATUS: Mfr. by Sormani
DIMENSIONS: W 29″ (73.7 cm),
D 30¾″ (78.1 cm),
H 26¾″ (67.9 cm)

Joe Colombo's Additional System consists of jersey-covered polyurethane slice-shaped sections in six different sizes. They can be combined to form chairs or sofas by means of aluminum clamps and a base bar. Although some think the system, which comes with a complementing plastic table, "too eccentric" to be used in homes, it meets the needs of many commercial clients by providing a great deal of flexibility without sacrificing good design.

BASTIANO SOFA AND SETTEE, 1969

DESIGNER: Tobia Scarpa (b. 1935)
COUNTRY: Italy
STATUS: Mfr. by Knoll International
DIMENSIONS: Settee: W 59¼"
(150.5 cm) D 32" (81.2 cm),
H 27" (68.5 cm);
Sofa: W 83½" (212.1 cm),
D 32" (81.2 cm), H 27" (68.5 cm)

Tobia Scarpa, architect and industrial designer, trained at Venice University. He and his wife Afra opened their own office in 1960 in Montebelluna, where they design a range of domestic products from glassware to furniture. This handsome collection has an exposed frame of oak, walnut, rosewood, or Honduras mahogany in a variety of finishes. The upholstery is leather. Deceptively simple in design, Bastiano is very well crafted of very high-quality materials—typical of the post-International Style in Italy.

MODELLO 780, 1966

DESIGNER: Gianfranco Frattini
COUNTRY: Italy
STATUS: Mfr. by Cassina
DIMENSIONS: Diameter 16½"
(42 cm), H 15¼" (39 cm)

Modello 780, designed by Gianfranco Frattini, is an innovative set of stacking tables in graduated heights. The legs of the tables are wood; the tops are thick and round. They stack compactly and neatly into a cylinder with the legs nestling in graduated sizes against each other in a space-saving arrangement.

TOGA CHAIR, 1968

DESIGNER: Sergio Mazza (b. 1931)
COUNTRY: Italy
STATUS: Not in production

Sergio Mazza was trained as an architect and opened his own office in 1956. He has been a member of the jury at the Milan Triennale since 1954. Toga is a single piece of fi-berglass reinforced with polyester and formed with a hot press. It is made only in red, white, black, and orange. Mazza presented it first at the Milan International Furniture Exhibition in 1969, where it was widely acclaimed. The Toga Chair can be stacked. It was formerly manufactured by Artemide.

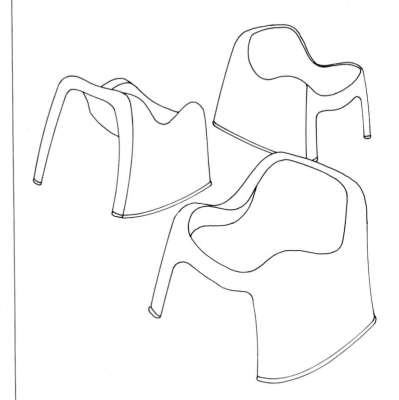

CHAIR 925, 1966

DESIGNERS: Afra (b. 1937)
and Tobia Scarpa
COUNTRY: Italy
STATUS: Mfr. by Cassina
DIMENSIONS: W 26″ (66 cm), D 25″
(63.5 cm), H 27¼″ (69.2 cm),
SH 13½″ (34.3 cm)

Afra and Tobia Scarpa work together out of their own office in Montebelluna. This chair was first shown in 1966 at the Milan International Furniture Fair. Its frame is made of ash or walnut, supporting a molded plywood back and seat. The upholstery is saddle-stitched leather or fabric in red or black over foam rubber. It is low to the ground and comfortably formed with rounded edges. A narrow space on the seat back provides lightness.

PLIA CHAIR, 1969

DESIGNER: Giancarlo Piretti
COUNTRY: Italy
STATUS: Mfr. by Krueger
DIMENSIONS: W 18½" (47 cm),
D 19¾" (50.2 cm), H 29"
(73.7 cm), SH 17½" (44.6 cm)

The Plia Chair is a modern adaptation of the simple wooden folding chair. Lightweight and relatively inexpensive, Plia is both functional and aesthetically appealing. It folds to a width of only one inch, excluding the hub, and neatly stacks. Made of cast aluminum with a seat and back of clear or opaque plastic in several pastel colors, Plia also has a companion table and armchair.

SOLUS, 1967

DESIGNER: Gae Aulenti
(b. 1927)
COUNTRY: Italy
STATUS: Mfr. by Zanotta
DIMENSIONS: W 21¾"
(55.2 cm), D 21¾" (55.2 cm),
H 25¾" (65.4 cm)

Gae Aulenti's Solus is made of plastic-coated tubular steel lacquered in any of a number of different colors. The round seat is padded and covered with a circular patterned fabric complementing the circle theme. Solus is a descendent of the Thonet B-9 Chair (page 13). Its bright finishes and upholstery are what make it distinctive. Aulenti is an architect, an industrial designer, and a stage designer as well as a furniture designer.

SASSI (ROCKS), 1967

DESIGNER: Piero Gilardi (b. 1900)
COUNTRY: Italy
STATUS: Mfr. by Gufram
DIMENSIONS: Variable

The Rocks are a provocative example of creative Italian design: They are seats of rock-shaped foam covered with fabric that looks like granite, complete with little flecks of mica shining here and there. Smaller rocks, which can be used as pillows, are intended to extend the metaphor—placed near the rock seats to make them look like the real thing.

BLOW CHAIR, 1967

DESIGNERS: Scolari: Donato D'Urbino; Paolo Lomazzi; Jonathan De Pas (all born in the 1930s)
COUNTRY: Italy
STATUS: Mfr. by Zanotta
DIMENSIONS: W 47¼" (120 cm), D 39¼" (99.7 cm), H 33" (83.8 cm), SH 15" (38.1 cm)

Scolari is a team of architects and industrial designers who have worked from their own office in Milan since the mid-1960s. Their inflatable Blow Chair is made from polyvinylchloride film. It is the first Italian inflatable chair in mass production. It is available in four colors.

SACCO, 1969

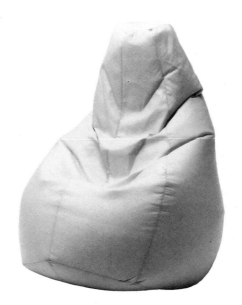

DESIGNERS: Design Studio/Piero Gatti; Cesare Paolini; Franco Teodoro (all born in the 1940s)
COUNTRY: Italy
STATUS: Mfr. by Zanotta; Dist. by ICF
DIMENSIONS: D 35½″ (90.1 cm), H 50¼″ (127.6 cm)

Sacco is lightweight, comfortable, and suitable for use on any surface, bumpy or smooth—a lot of fun. It was an accidental creation, a result of serendipity, when polystyrene pellets used on a production line were thrown into a bag, and these designers noticed. The forerunner of the "bean-bag" chair, Sacco is made of approximately 12 million pellets sewn into a leather or plastic cover. Although it looks precarious, Sacco is really quite stable.

SERIES UP, 1969

DESIGNER: Gaetano Pesce (b. 1939)
COUNTRY: Italy
STATUS: Mfr. by B & B Italia
DIMENSIONS: Up 5: W 38½″ (97.8 cm), D 38½″ (97.8 cm), H 25½″ (64.8 cm), SH 10½″ (26.7 cm)

Gaetano Pesce trained in architecture and graphic design at Venice University and opened his own office in Padua. He was a founding member of design firm Group N. The Up Series is made of polyurethane foam with nylon jersey covers. Up 1 has two buttons deep into the seat to hold the upholstery taut. The six pieces are each compressed to one-tenth their volumes and shipped sealed in plastic envelopes inside flat boxes. When the packages are opened, the pieces pop back into shape.

DONDOLO ROCKING CHAIR, 1969

DESIGNERS: Cesare Leonardi (b. 1935); Franca Stagi (b. 1937)
COUNTRY: Italy
STATUS: Mfr. by Bellato
DIMENSIONS: W 15¾" (40 cm), D 69" (175 cm), H 30¾" (78 cm)

Architects and industrial designers Leonardi and Stagi opened an office together in Modena, Italy, in 1961. One of their objectives when they created Dondolo was that the chair be a work of art when not in use. As a rocker, Dondolo is unique because it rocks even the feet, like a Ferris wheel seat. It is made of molded fiberglass and is available in three colors.

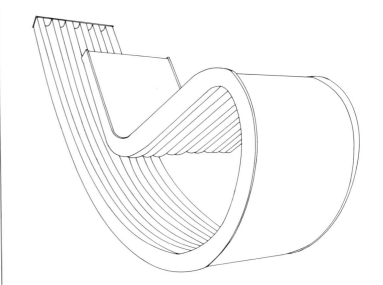

CHAIR 932/2, 1967

DESIGNER: Mario Bellini (b. 1935)
COUNTRY: Italy
STATUS: Not in production

Prominent Italian architect, educator, and industrial and furniture designer Mario Bellini opened his office in Milan in 1962. Chair 932/2 is made of interchangeable component cushions. Injection-molded polyurethane with Dacron padding and covered in leather, they can be arranged to create a one, two, or three seat chair or sofa. To connect the cushions, Bellini used a leather belt passed through flat leather loops stitched onto the upholstery. Chair 932/2 was inspired by Le Corbusier's LC-2 Petit and Confort Chair (page 70), but it has no steel frame or springs. Chair 932/2 was formerly manufactured by Cassina and distributed by Atelier International.

COLOMBO CHAIR 4860, 1967

DESIGNER: Joe Colombo
COUNTRY: Italy
STATUS: Mfr. by Kartell
DIMENSIONS: W 17¼″ (43.8 cm),
D 19¾″ (50.2 cm), H 28½″
(72.4 cm), SH 16¼″ (41.3 cm)

Colombo's Chair 4860 is the first all-plastic (ABS) chair to be made by the sophisticated, but inexpensive method of injection molding. The chair comes in two heights (two different leg lengths attach to the feet), and is available in five colors. It can be stacked. Chair 4860 was designed in 1967 and put into production a year later.

SORIANA GROUP, 1970

DESIGNERS: Afra and Tobia Scarpa
COUNTRY: Italy
STATUS: Mfr. by Cassina;
Dist. by Atelier International
DIMENSIONS: Armless Chair: W 35″
(88.9 cm), D 41.3″ (104.9 cm),
H 28.3″ (71.9 cm), SH 17″
(42.8 cm);
Three-Seat Sofa: W 98.5″
(250.2 cm)

The Soriana Group is a luxurious seating group. Shown here is an armless chair, a two-seat sofa, and a three-seat sofa.

The group also includes an ottoman and a chaise lounge. It has only a small wood base supporting polyurethane foam covered in soft Dacron fiberfill and a loose-fitting fabric or leather upholstery. The shape of Soriana is maintained by two chrome-plated steel wire clips arranged on the front and back sections. The chair won the Gold Medal at the Milan Triennale and is included in the Permanent Collection of The Museum of Modern Art in New York City.

World War II wreaked havoc in Europe. England's economy was devastated; Germany had to rebuild; France, too, had been invaded and needed to concentrate on recovery. Perhaps these conditions explain why, throughout the 1950s, there was relatively little innovation anywhere except in Italy and Scandinavia.

In Germany, designers worked primarily in Post-International Style, using new materials—as Italians were doing with so much innovation and invention—but staying within the philosophical and aesthetic boundaries laid down by the Bauhaus in the 1920s. Some beautiful pieces emerged, and some innovations as well—the wall unit being one of the most interesting. At this time, Americans like George Nelson were working on component furniture and the idea of storage walls. The Post-International Style, as used by Hans Gugelot and Jürgen Lange, made these units into works of high style. In Brazil a designer named Sergio Rodriguez also worked in the Post-International Style; his Sherriff Chair is a relaxed version with a hammock-type design.

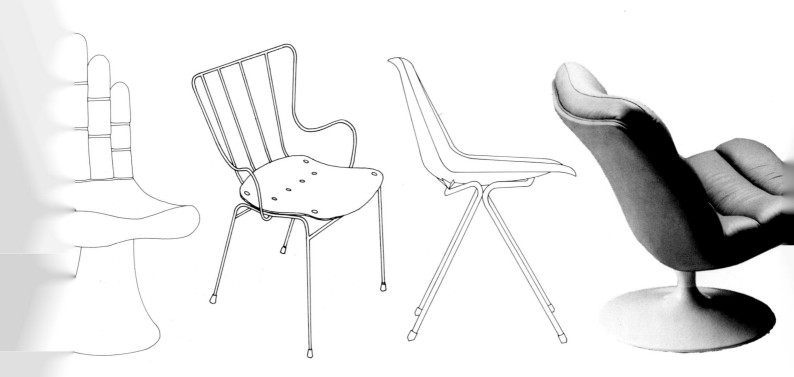

FRANCE, ENGLAND,

In England, the so-called Utility Programme produced standardized furniture made of basic materials in an unadventurous fashion. Of note was Ernest Race, who worked innovatively in the 1950s to produce furniture from salvaged aircraft materials. And then in 1951 an exhibition called the Festival of Britain stimulated designers like Robin Day, Clive Latimer, and Ernest Race. They explored new materials in a lightly scaled manner.

French designers of the period redirected the International Style into pieces with flowing organic lines. They too used new materials—rubberized canvas, fiberglass shells—and they paid attention to good craftsmanship. Olivier Mourgue introduced a surrealist note with his sculpture-chaise Bouloum, made in the shape of a human. In Mexico, a little earlier, Pedro Freideberg had designed a hand-shaped chair.

While it is true that from the late 1950s and through the 1960s the dynamic centers of European design were in Scandinavia and in Italy, designers throughout Europe achieved high standards of beauty, intelligence, and style.

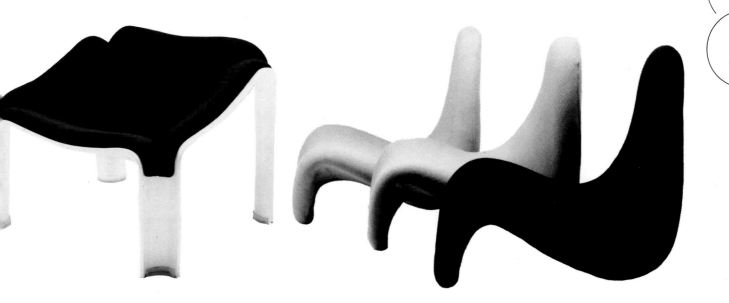

M 125 MODULAR GROUP, 1953

DESIGNER: Hans Gugelot
(1920–1965)
COUNTRY: Germany
STYLE: Post-International/
Neo-Functionalism
STATUS: Mfr. by Baresel-Bofinger
DIMENSIONS: Variable

Hans Gugelot was a member of the Hochschule für Gestaltung, an avant-garde design school near Ulm, Germany, that focused on updating the Bauhaus approach by making it relevant to postwar society. M 125 is constructed of metal rods with gray plastic sides and shelves. Dark afromosia wood trim provides striking outlines. Components may be arranged to suit the user. There are bookcases, cupboards, room dividers, and wardrobes.

BEHR 1600 WALL SYSTEM, 1970–1971

DESIGNER: Jürgen Lange
COUNTRY: Germany
STATUS: Not in production

Jürgen Lange is one of Germany's most prominent designers. His cabinet wall system, made of pure white polyester, is free-standing and movable. Components include storage cupboards, desks, fold-down tables, beds on hinges, shelves, and drawers—allowing the user to meet all kinds of needs. Formerly manufactured by Behr for Interlübke and distributed by ICF.

MEXICO

HAND CHAIR, 1963

DESIGNER: Pedro Freideberg
(b. 1937)
COUNTRY: Italy/Mexico
STYLE: Pop Furniture/Surrealistic
STATUS: Handcrafted
DIMENSIONS: Available in both
adult and child sizes

Italian-born designer and sculptor Pedro Freideberg migrated to Mexico. He created this piece of Pop Art sculpture that also functions as a chair. It is handmade of wood and offered in gold leaf, natural, or lacquer finishes. The chair is relatively inexpensive.

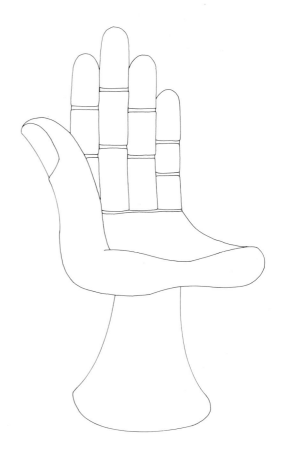

SHERRIFF CHAIR, 1958

DESIGNER: Sergio Rodriguez
COUNTRY: Brazil
STATUS: Mfr. by OCA

The Sherriff Chair is made like a hammock—the large cushion seat and back are suspended from interlaced leather straps pegged into a teak frame. Its appearance is casual and inviting yet formal and imposing. It is very comfortable as well.

ANTELOPE CHAIR, 1950

DESIGNER: Ernest Race
(1913–1963)
COUNTRY: England
STYLE: Early Postwar Modern
STATUS: Not in production

In 1945 Ernest Race founded Ernest Race Furniture with a tool and die manufacturer in order to apply modern engineering techniques to making furniture. Antelope was one of their designs. It has a painted steel-rod frame with a plywood seat. At the famous Festival of Britain in 1951, the Antelope Chair was exhibited as an outdoor chair. It won a Silver Medal at the Milan Triennale in 1954. Another design of Race's, the BA Chair of 1945, was made of cast aluminum—aircraft salvage. It won a Gold Medal at the Milan Triennale in 1954.

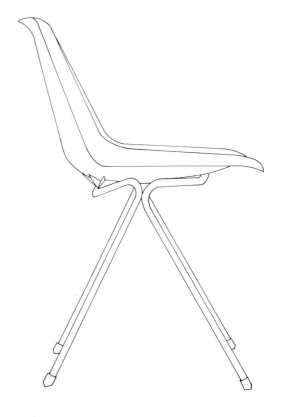

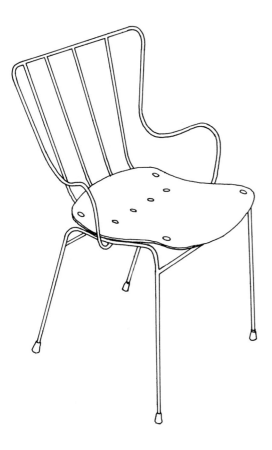

POLYPROP CHAIR, 1963

DESIGNER: Robin Day (b. 1915)
COUNTRY: England
STATUS: Mfr. by Source One
Dist. by John Stuart International
DIMENSIONS: W 20½″ (52.1 cm),
D 20″ (50.8 cm), H 29″ (73.7 cm),
SH 15½″ (39.4 cm)

In 1948 British designer Robin Day received first prize, with Clive Latimer, in a competition called Low-Cost Furniture Design, sponsored by The Museum of Modern Art in New York City, for a wall storage unit. Later, Day designed the Polyprop Chair. Made of polypropylene, it is cheap and strong, and it can be made by injection molding. It has a one-piece seat back that can be mounted on various kinds of frames and is stackable. It comes in many colors: charcoal and light gray, orange-red, yellow ocher, olive, royal blue, and others by special order, or it can be fully upholstered.

POLKA DOT CHILD'S CHAIR, 1964

DESIGNER: Peter Murdoch (b. 1940)
COUNTRY: England
STATUS: Not in production;
Collection, Victoria and
Albert Museum, London

The Polka Dot Chair is made of washable polyethylene-coated laminated paperboard suitable for mass production and is relatively inexpensive. The design is simple, but three different papers and five laminations are necessary. The chair can be shipped in a pile of 800, which measures only four feet high. Peter Murdoch formed his own company to produce the Polka Dot Chair.

CHAIR 506, 1968

DESIGNER: Geoffrey Harcourt
(b. 1935)
COUNTRY: England
STATUS: Mfr. by Artifort
DIMENSIONS: W 27½" (69.9 cm),
D 28¼" (72 cm), H 27½"
(69.9 cm), SH 15¾" (40 cm)

Geoffrey Harcourt trained at High Wycombe and at the Royal College of Art. After spending a year in the United States, he joined the Artifort Design Group. Chair 506, part of the 500 Series, is a pedestal chair with a pleasant tilt and comfortable upholstery.

RIBBON CHAIR 582, 1965

DESIGNER: Pierre Paulin (b. 1927)
COUNTRY: France
STATUS: Mfr. by Artifort
Dist. by Krueger
DIMENSIONS: W 39½" (100.3 cm),
D 29¾" (75.6 cm), H 27½"
(69.9 cm), SH 10¾" (27.3 cm)

Pierre Paulin was on the research team for Mobilier National in Paris as a consultant to Artifort. His furniture has won several Gold Medals at the Brussels Expo and the Milan Triennale. In 1969, the Ribbon Chair received the AID Design Award. It is constructed of a tension-held rubber sheet over a tubular metal frame with jersey-covered latex foam upholstery. A lacquered wood base supports the frame.

CHAIR 300, 1965–1966

DESIGNER: Pierre Paulin
COUNTRY: France
STATUS: Mfr. by Artifort;
Dist. by Krueger
DIMENSIONS: W 31¾" (80.5 cm),
D 28" (71.1 cm), H 23¾"
(60.3 cm), SH 11" (27.9 cm)

One of France's outstanding living designers, Pierre Paulin has created a number of classic pieces. Chair 300, in the Post-International Style, is comfortable and handsome. Made of a fiberglass shell with removable jersey-covered latex foam upholstery, it is available in three shell colors. Chair 300 was first shown at the Utrecht Furniture Exhibition in 1967.

BOULOUM, 1969

DESIGNER: Olivier Mourgue
(b. 1939)
COUNTRY: France
STATUS: Mfr. by Arconas
Corporation
DIMENSIONS: W 26″ (66 cm),
D 57″ (144.8 cm), H 24″ (61 cm)

The whimsical image of a reclining man is captured by Olivier Mourgue in Bouloum. It is a chaise made of fiberglass with a gel coating for outdoor use, or of steel tubing with upholstery for indoor use. The outdoor model has a white surface with a black underside and is slightly smaller than the indoor model, which comes in 29 colors. A Bouloum room divider is also available.

CHAIR 577, 1967

DESIGNER: Pierre Paulin
COUNTRY: France
STATUS: Mfr. by Artifort;
Dist. by Krueger
DIMENSIONS: W 33½″ (85 cm),
D 35½″ (90 cm), H 24″ (61 cm),
SH 13⅜″ (34.7 cm)

Chair 577, sometimes called Birds in Flight, is part of the Permanent Collections at New York's The Museum of Modern Art and the Musée des Arts Décoratifs in Paris. The curving form of the chair is repeated in its matching ottoman. Made of a high-frequency pressed-wood shell and a tubular frame, Chair 577 is upholstered in rubber and an elasticized fabric available in a wide range of colors.

THE 1970s

The 1970s in Europe saw a continuation, in principle, of design trends of the postwar period. Pop furniture, for example, continued to enjoy a certain degree of popularity into the 1970s. The Italians focused on innovative materials while refining a Post-International Style. And yet some new concepts emerged. The Primate Kneeling Stool is a unique approach to sitting; the Appoggio Chair is a unique approach to supported standing. Modular seating steadily gained in importance, and the various modules became increasingly imaginative.

In the United States, designers returned to

more traditional materials in their pursuit of refining the Post-International Style. Wicker and rattan became important, as did unupholstered wood. Modular furniture bloomed too, winding with abandon in serpentine curves around American living rooms of the 1970s.

Toward the end of the decade, the Arts and Crafts value of fine craftsmanship appeared once again in England and in the United States with the Craft Revival Movement. Furniture from this movement is entirely handmade in designers' studios. Designers such as Sam Maloof, Rupert Williamson, and Judy Kensley McKie led the Craft Revival Movement into the 1980s.

PRIMATE KNEELING STOOL, 1970

DESIGNER: Achille Castiglioni
COUNTRY: Italy
STATUS: Mfr. by ICF
DIMENSIONS: W 19″ (48.3 cm),
D 31½″ (80 cm), H 18½″ (47 cm)

Designed in 1970 by the prominent Italian designer Achille Castiglioni, the Primate Kneeling Stool again became popular in the 1980s because of the physical fitness movement. At first, one hardly knows how to sit in this chair. The knees and legs rest on the bottom level, and the smaller upper unit, upholstered in leather or Naugahyde, is for sitting upon. The surprisingly comfortable posture that results—the sitter's hips are tipped back—helps prevent backaches.

TYPING CHAIR MODELL Z9r, 1970–1971

DESIGNER: Ettore Sottsass Jr.
(b. 1918)
COUNTRY: Austria/Italy
STATUS: Mfr. by Olivetti Synthesis
DIMENSIONS: W 22½″ (57 cm),
D 22½″ (57 cm),
H 18½–32″ (47–81.2 cm)

Ettore Sottsass Jr., although born in Austria, is primarily known as an Italian designer and was responsible for the Memphis movement (pages 182–183) of the 1980s. But before Memphis, Sottsass worked for Olivetti, designing typewriters and office furnishings. This plastic swivel chair is upholstered in polyfoam with fabric covers. The plastic frame is a brilliant yellow. The chair can be used as a stool by turning down the back; both seat and back heights are adjustable.

GAUDI CHAIR, 1970

DESIGNER: Vico Magistretti
COUNTRY: Italy
STATUS: Mfr. by Artemide
DIMENSIONS: W 28½″ (72.4 cm),
D 25½″ (64.8 cm),
H 26¾″ (67.9 cm)

The Gaudi armchair is made of preimpregnated resin. Somewhat similar to Sergio Mazza's Toga Chair of 1968 (page 136), the Gaudi has a flowing form with distinctive vertical grooves in the front legs and elliptical perforations in the back above the rear legs. It is available in a number of colors.

STACKING STORAGE THING, 1970

DESIGNER: Anna Castelli Ferrieri
COUNTRY: Italy
STATUS: Mfr. by Kartell
DIMENSIONS: Variable

Anna Castelli Ferrieri works dramatically with new materials. She is especially noted for her use of rigid ABS plastic. This circular Stacking Storage Thing is a container for storing small items. It is available in a range of colors. Designed in 1969, it went into production the following year.

APPOGGIO CHAIR, 1971

DESIGNER: Claudio
Salocchi (b. 1934)
COUNTRY: Italy
STATUS: Mfr. by Sormani
DIMENSIONS: Adjustable

The uniquely slender Appoggio Chair was made for sitting down while in a standing position. Perfect for use in kitchens, or for cashiering, clerking, and so on, Appoggio has a graceful metal support base that can be adjusted to suit the sitter.

ANFIBIO SOFA, 1971

DESIGNER: Alessandro
Becchi (b. 1946)
COUNTRY: Italy
STATUS: Mfr. by Giovannetti
DIMENSIONS: W 43½"–94½"
(110.5–240 cm), D 37¾"–38½"
(95.9–97.8 cm), H 25½" (64.8 cm)

Anfibio is a sofabed. The conversion is made simply by unfolding the sofa, which contains a mattress. The sofa is held in its folded position by nylon zippers and leather straps. Its substructure is made of steel covered with polyurethane, and it is upholstered in either leather or fabric. This piece has been a popular choice for small areas and has sparked a number of new design ideas to replace the traditional convertible sofa.

LUNARIO TABLE, 1972

DESIGNER: Cini Boeri (b. 1924)
COUNTRY: Italy
STATUS: Mfr. by Knoll International
DIMENSIONS: W 59" (149.9 cm),
D 44" (111.8 cm), H 15¾" (40 cm)
or 27½" (69.9 cm)

Cini Boeri is one of Italy's most influential designers. The Lunario Table is cantilevered. Its base and counterweights are made of polished steel and its top is half-inch tempered glass, or white or black plastic with an asymmetrically placed steel cap.

MARALUNGA, 1973

DESIGNER: Vico Magistretti
COUNTRY: Italy
STATUS: Mfr. by Cassina;
Dist. by Atelier International
DIMENSIONS: W 38½″ (98 cm),
D 33½″ (85.1 cm), H 28½″–41″
(72.1–104.1 cm), SH 17″ (42.9 cm)

Maralunga was included in *Fortune* magazine's 1977 list of the 25 best-designed prod-ucts—it was the only piece of furniture included. The arm-chair, ottoman, and sofa all have steel frames and black ABS bases. The padding is polyurethane foam with Dacron, and the upholstery is fabric or leather. Magistretti made Maralunga unique by using a movable headrest; the sofa has individual headrests for each seat.

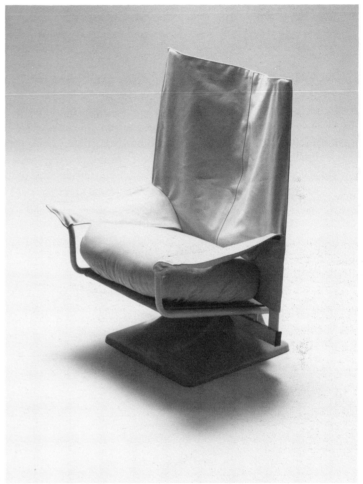

AEO, 1973

DESIGNER: Archizoom/
Paolo Deganello (b. 1940)
COUNTRY: Italy
STATUS: Mfr. by Cassina
DIMENSIONS: W 30⅞″ (78.4 cm),
D 27¼″ (69.2 cm),
H 41″ (104.1 cm)

In 1966 Paolo Deganello founded Archizoom, a studio in Florence, with designers Branzi, Corretti, and Mo-rozzi. It closed in 1974. AEO is one of Deganello's best-known collaborative efforts. It has a gray durethane base, a lacquered steel frame in white or gray, with or without arms, and a padded seat and back covered with leather or fabric upholstery.

NO. 1000 JOE LOUNGE CHAIR, 1970

DESIGNERS: Design Studio/
DePas; D'Urbino; Lomazzi
STYLE: Pop Furniture
COUNTRY: Italy
STATUS: Mfr. by Poltronova
DIMENSIONS: W 65"
(165 cm), D 42" (106.7 cm),
H 34" (86.4 cm),
SH 16½" (42 cm)

The Joe Lounge Chair is an amusing example of pop furniture. The creation was inspired quite literally by a quote from America's famed furniture designer, Charles Eames: "A chair should welcome the body—like a well-used baseball glove." In honor of Joe DiMaggio, the great baseball hero, the baseball glove form was nicknamed Batting Joe, or just Joe. The comfortable fielder's glove is made of molded reinforced urethane foam and is upholstered in natural glove leather.

THE IONIC, 1972

DESIGNERS: Studio 65/Piero Gatti;
Casare Paolini; Franco Teodoro
(all born in the 1940s)
COUNTRY: Italy
STYLE: Pop Furniture
STATUS: Mfr. by Gufram
DIMENSIONS: Variable

The Studio 65 design team is located in Turin, Italy. This seat, called Capitello in Italian, is really a Pop Art sculpture as well as a chair. It is based on the Ionic column of ancient Greece. Its form is like a rolled scroll topped with curved ram's horns. It is made of soft polyurethane foam. Some designers feel that no more than one Ionic piece should be used in a design.

EASY EDGES, 1972–1980s

DESIGNER: Frank O. Gehry (b. 1929)
COUNTRY: United States
STATUS: Not in production

Canadian-born Frank Gehry has been practicing architecture out of his California office since the early 1970s. He used corrugated fiberboard laminated with epoxy for this sculptural furniture. It was originally produced by Cheru Enterprises, a Swiss firm. There are plans to reintroduce it.

CAB CHAIR, 1977

DESIGNER: Mario Bellini (b. 1935)
COUNTRY: Italy
STATUS: Mfr. by Cassina;
Dist. by Atelier International
DIMENSIONS: Armless Chair:
W 20½" (54.5 cm), D 18½"
(47 cm), H 32¼" (81.9 cm)

Mario Bellini's Cab Chair has a frame of enamelled steel with saddle-stitched upholstery that zips into place over the frame. An armchair and settee made the same way are also available. Although Bellini is an architect, much of his work has been in industrial design. He has won the Compasso d'Oro five times, and several of his designs are included in the Permanent Collection of The Museum of Modern Art in New York City.

BASKET CHAIR 8043, 1970s

DESIGNER: Harvey Probber (b. 1922)
COUNTRY: United States
STATUS: Mfr. by Harvey Probber
DIMENSIONS: W 22″ (55.9 cm),
D 22″ (55.9 cm), H 31″ (78.7 cm),
AH 26¾″ (67.3 cm),
SH 18″ (45.7 cm)

This chair is made of natural wicker woven over a welded steel frame and positioned on a cantilevered base. Loose foam seat and back cushions are covered in fabric or leather. The chair is also available in Polywich®, a vinyl-based synthetic wicker made for heavy use indoors or out. Harvey Probber has adapted Breuer's Cesca Chair (page 64)—using ancient weaving techniques to renew a modern style. Probber, in the 1930s, was one of the first to design modular seating; that was in the 1930s.

OFFENBURG PARK CHAIR, 1971

DESIGNER: Heinz Wirth
COUNTRY: Germany
STATUS: Dist. by Kroin
DIMENSIONS: W 23½″ (59.7 cm),
D 24⅝″ (62.6 cm), H 32½″
(82.6 cm), SH 17¾″ (45.1 cm),
AH 26½″ (67.3 cm)

The Offenburg Park Chair and garden furniture was developed for the 1972 Olympics and was the winner of eight international design awards. The chairs are made in a wide range of designs, some of which are modular, can be used in a variety of locations, and can be stacked. Available in white or green, they are made of tubular steel with a wire grid seat and back specially developed to withstand abuse in or out of doors.

TRIANGLE CHAIR, 1974

DESIGNER: Robert De Fuccio
COUNTRY: United States
STATUS: Mfr. by Stow/Davis
DIMENSIONS: W 21¾″
(55.2 cm), D 21¾″ (55.2 cm),
H 21½″ (54.5 cm),
AH 26¼″ (66.7 cm)

The Triangle Chair is made of laminated hardwood—currently walnut or oak. Its seat and back are molded plywood covered with flame-retardant polyfoam or with caning. It was designed by industrial designer Robert De Fuccio, who opened his own firm after working for Knoll International for 10 years. De Fuccio's objective is to create beautiful chairs that are "logical, simple, distinctive, strong, light-weight, and comfortable."

CLUB TUB, 1970s

DESIGNER: Joan Burgasser (b. 1934)
COUNTRY: United States
STATUS: Mfr. by Thonet Industries
DIMENSIONS: W 27″ (68.5 cm),
D 25″ (63.5 cm), H 29½″
(74.9 cm), SH 17″ (42.8 cm),
AH 24″ (61 cm)

The Club Tub (*left*), designed by Joan Burgasser when she was vice president of design for Thonet Industries, is based on Anton Lorenz's chair of 1926 (*right*). The frame of Club Tub is a continuous length of 14-gauge chrome-plated tubular steel one inch in diameter. The cantilevered seat and back are upholstered urethane with an elastic strap seat base. Variations of both designs are available from Thonet Industries.

NONSTOP SOFA, 1972

DESIGNERS: Eleonore Peduzzi-Riva;
with Heinz Ulrich; Klaus
Vogt; Veli Berger
COUNTRY: Italy/Switzerland
STATUS: Dist. by
Stendig International
DIMENSIONS: W 9" (22.7 cm),
D 84" (213.4 cm), H 30¾"
(101 cm), SH 16" (40.6 cm)

Nonstop is potentially endless. It is a series of accordianlike modules linked together to form curves or straight sofas, chairs, settees. The understructure is molded foam reinforced with metal and wood and covered in a choice of tan or brown carpeting. The upper section is made of Dacron-wrapped urethane foam upholstered in Swiss leather or suede. The sofa is available with right and left arm components and high or low backs.

CHADWICK MODULAR SEATING, 1974

DESIGNER: Don Chadwick (b. 1936)
COUNTRY: United States
STATUS: Mfr. by Herman Miller
DIMENSIONS: Variable

Chadwick Modular Seating, produced by Herman Miller since 1974, was selected by *Interior Design* as one of the 46 most influential furnishings of the past 50 years of modern design. There are five modules: a rectangular seat unit (usable as a chair), and four wedge types with concave or convex curves in two diameters (11'-7"; 9'-2"). The various units have attached bases and can be linked together in an undulated row. A deep fold where seat and back meet makes Chadwick Modular Seating unique.

SERIES SIT-DOWN, 1975

DESIGNER: Gaetano Pesce
COUNTRY: Italy
STATUS: Mfr. by Cassina
DIMENSIONS: Chair: W 45"
(114.3 cm),
D 34¾" (88.3 cm), H 28¾"
(73 cm), SH 17" (42.8 cm)

Pesce's Series Up (page 139) is in the permanent collection of the Victoria and Albert Museum in London; a Series Sit-Down chair is also in The Museum of Modern Art's Permanent Collection in New York City. The Sit-Down pieces are made of foam rubber with padding injected into a Dacron quilted cover. The bases of the chair and sofa are made of plywood. The collection also includes a sofa and an ottoman.

AULENTI COLLECTION, 1977

DESIGNER: Gae Aulenti (b. 1927)
COUNTRY: Italy
STATUS: Mfr. by Knoll International
DIMENSIONS: Two-Seat: W 64¼"
(163.2 cm), D 33¾" (85.7 cm),
H 30¼" (76.8 cm);
Three-Seat: W 87½" (222.3 cm)

Gae Aulenti is a professor, architect, and industrial designer. Her handsome Aulenti Collection consists of a lounge chair, a settee, a sofa, and dining and coffee tables. The frames of the group are made of extruded steel with a finish of light, medium, or dark metallic gray, black, or Amaranto. The upholstery is foam with a Dacron wrap over rubber and steel for both seat and back cushions. The tables come in a variety of sizes.

UNIVERSITY CHAIR, circa 1971

DESIGNER: Ward Bennett (b. 1917)
COUNTRY: United States
STATUS: Mfr. by Brickel Associates
DIMENSIONS: W 22¼" (56.5 cm),
D 24" (61 cm), H 32½"
(82.6 cm), SH 18" (45.7 cm),
AH 25¼" (64.1 cm)

The University Chair was designed by Ward Bennett for the Lyndon B. Johnson Library at the University of Texas in Austin. Carved from large blocks of solid ash, the chair is meticulously joined and finished to reveal the wood's distinctive grain. Although made entirely of unupholstered wood, the University Chair is remarkably comfortable. It is a simple yet sturdy and elegant chair.

3 TRE CHAIR, 1977–1978

DESIGNER: Angelo
Mangiarotti (b. 1921)
COUNTRY: Italy
STATUS: Mfr. by Skipper Italy
DIMENSIONS: W 21¾" (55.3 cm),
D 22½" (57 cm),
H 26½" (67.3 cm)

Angelo Mangiarotti's architectural approach to furniture has led him to design his fluid forms with attention to planning total environments. He also keeps comfort in mind. This elegant 3 Tre Chair, named for its three materials, has three legs made of solid walnut and a seat of steel and leather. It is available in three heights and is similar in design to the T-Chair of 1952 (page 120). Mangiarotti has practiced architecture, industrial design, and urban planning in Milan since 1955.

IL COLONNATO TABLES, 1977

DESIGNER: Mario Bellini
COUNTRY: Italy
STATUS: Mfr. by Cassina
DIMENSIONS: Square: 55¼"
(140.2 cm), H 28¾" (73.2 cm);
Round: Diameter 47.2" (119.9 cm),
H 28¾" (73.2 cm)

Il Colonnato Tables are made of marble supported by three, four, or five columns arranged in a suggested way or as desired. The columns, also marble, are cut from solid blocks in the Ionic style. After being polished, the marble tops are treated with highly durable epoxy resin to make a beige or black glossy coating. These tables are very heavy: the largest, 1320 pounds; the smallest, 905. Bellini received the 1978 Resources Council of Design Award for Il Colonnato. A year later Marco Zanuso designed the similar Basilio Table.

ROCKING CHAIR,
1970s–1980s

DESIGNER: Sam Maloof (b. 1916)
COUNTRY: United States
STYLE: Craft Revival
STATUS: Handcrafted

Californian Sam Maloof is an important promoter of the Craft Revival in the United States. As early as 1949, Maloof began designing and producing handcrafted furniture. He is best known for his rockers. His expert craftsmanship earned him the prestigious "Genius Grant" from the MacArthur Foundation.

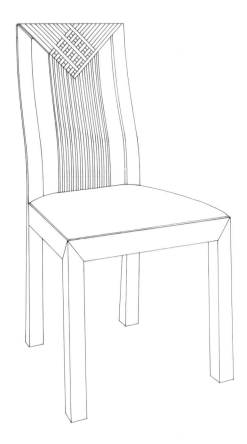

WILLIAMSON CHAIR,
late 1970s

DESIGNER: Rupert Williamson
COUNTRY: England
STYLE: Craft Revival
STATUS: Handcrafted

Rupert Williamson, one of England's most famous and talented designers, has been an important part of the Craft Revival Movement. This chair is made of maple and rosewood. It has a geometric, linear design that ends in a satisfying woven motif at the top of the back. Along with his contemporary John Makepeace, Williamson makes his high-quality pieces by hand.

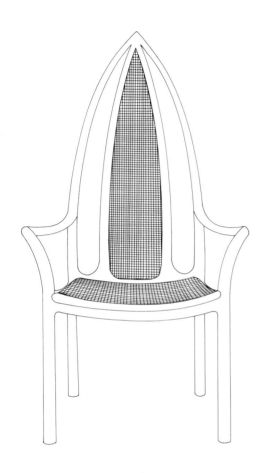

BENCH WITH HORSES, 1979

DESIGNER: Judy Kensley
McKie (b. 1944)
COUNTRY: United States
STYLE: Craft Revival
STATUS: Handcrafted;
Collection, Museum of Fine Arts,
Boston, purchased through funds
provided by the National Endowment
for the Arts and the
Deborah M. Noonan Foundation
DIMENSIONS: D 27″ (68.6 cm),
H 27¼″ (69.2 cm), L 60″ (152.5 cm)

One of America's most popular artist furniture designers, Judy Kensley McKie, of Somerville, Massachusetts, is known for her combination of fantasy and functionalism. The mahogany and leather Bench with Horses has corners with elongated stylized horse heads and wings on the side of the seat. Suggestive of classical mythology, the piece nevertheless has a distinctly twentieth-century feeling.

EBONY GOTHIC CHAIR, 1978

DESIGNER: John Makepeace
(b. 1939)
COUNTRY: England
STYLE: Craft Revival
STATUS: Handcrafted by
John Makepeace Designs

The value of handcrafted furniture stressed by the Arts and Crafts Movement in the nineteenth century has been stressed again by the Craft Revival Movement in the United States and England. In 1977, John Makepeace founded a school for designers and craftsmen at Parnham House in Dorset, England. This chair is made of 2,000 pieces. The Gothic style appealed to Arts and Crafts designers, too.

THE 1980s

he 1980s have seen both the advanced use of new techniques and materials (developed largely by the Italians) and a continuation of interest in fine craftsmanship.

Classic Modernism is still a design force, albeit with modified, much less geometric lines. Form and function in this style are still united, and simplicity and purity still hold sway. Art Furniture is popular again. The Craft Revival of the 1970s continues to engage designers who work with wood in the old hand methods while incorporating new design ideas. The High-Tech style also continues to be very popular throughout the 1980s. By using the latest technology and materials, high-tech designers achieved a clean, metallic, and utilitarian yet elegant look.

A movement called Ergonomics—combining high styling with high technology—has become

especially important in office furnishings. Furniture made in this style is not only adjustable in just about every direction, it is equipped with computer memory of the sitter's needs as well.

Freshest looking of the many styles of the 1980s are Memphis and related Post-Modern, and yet these styles are derived from Art Deco and the 1950s, and, in Robert Venturi's case, even Chippendale. Designers since 1980 have approached furniture from the radical standpoint of rash disregard for comfort: chairs and tables so fierce and forbidding one dreads to use them. Designers also have grinned playfully through their work: outrageously bright colors, exaggerated forms, cartoon shapes and sizes. Still, in Memphis pieces, we can see the old elements of De Stijl in those discrete shapes and brilliant colors. Only the wit is 1980s.

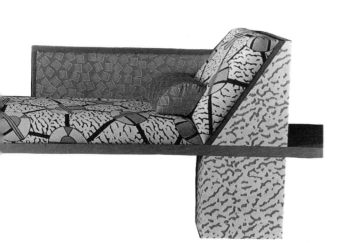

CHAIRS, 1982–1983

DESIGNER: Philippe Starck
(b. 1949)
COUNTRY: France
STATUS: Mfr. by ICF
DIMENSIONS: Variable

Philippe Starck, considered something of an *enfant terrible*, designs clubs and discos as well as furniture. These chairs (*left*) were designed for his Café Costes in Paris. Doctor Sonderbar (*center*) was inspired by the pilot seat of a dirigible aircraft. Its frame is made of steel tubing and is available in a nickel- or silver-plate or black or green epoxy-coated finish. Richard III (*right*) gives the impression of an overstuffed armchair.

87 SECONDA ARMCHAIR, 1982

DESIGNER: Mario Botta (b. 1943)
COUNTRY: Switzerland
STATUS: Mfr. by ICF
DIMENSIONS: W 20½″ (52.1 cm),
D 22¾″ (57.8 cm), H 28¼″
(71.8 cm), SH 18½″ (47 cm),
AH 26″ (66 cm)

Mario Botta received international attention for his residential architecture throughout the 1980s. He is also well known for his furniture. The Seconda's frame is made of tubular steel. It has a seat of perforated sheet metal finished with black or silver epoxy. The back is charcoal gray expanded polyurethane without upholstery. In addition to Seconda, Botta's work for ICF includes the 86 Prima Armless Chair, the 922 Terzo Table, and the 22 Quarta Chair. His 1985 collection for Alias in Italy included the Quinta, the 22 Quarta, the Prince, and the King and Queen—all of which received rave notices worldwide.

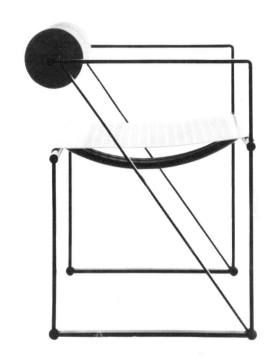

ALUMINUM CHAIR, 1981

DESIGNER: Scott Burton (b. 1939)
COUNTRY: United States
STATUS: Produced by designer;
Collection, Max Protetch Gallery

Comfort is not the idea of this chair designed by Scott Burton. He is a sculptor and conceptual artist whose work has been seen at the High Styles: Twentieth Century American Design exhibition at the Whitney Museum of American Art in New York City and elsewhere around the United States. Made of aluminum perforated with stylish circles, this chair seems to dare to be sat in.

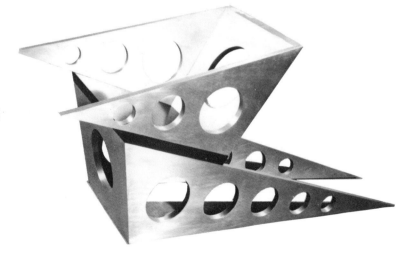

SOF-TECH COLLECTION SIDE CHAIR, 1979

DESIGNER: David Rowland (b. 1924)
COUNTRY: United States
STATUS: Mfr. by Thonet Industries
DIMENSIONS: W 19¾″ (50.2 cm),
D 20½″ (52.1 cm), H 29¾″
(75.6 cm), SH 18″ (45.7 cm)

The Sof-Tech Collection won the 1979 IBD Gold Medal Award for Special Seating. Made of the patented Soflex® material, a network of coated springs, the seats and backs allow air to circulate around the body while providing the comfort of support that moves with the sitter. Both arm and side chairs can be stacked. The frame is made of tubular steel ⅞″ in diameter in six colors, brass plating, or polished chrome plating. Also available are a counter-height chair and an interlocking system for linking chairs together.

NETWORK CHAIR, 1985

DESIGNER: Niels Jorgen Haugesen
COUNTRY: Denmark
STATUS: Mfr. by ICF
DIMENSIONS: W 19½″ (49.5 cm),
D 17½″ (44.6 cm),
H 30½″ (77.5 cm)

Niels Jorgen Haugesen's work represents a trend toward integrating the latest materials technology and newest construction techniques with Scandinavian design. The Network Chair is designed for indoor and outdoor use. Made of a lightweight, chrome-plated, solid-bar steel with a seat and back of black, gray, or white epoxy-coated perforated steel, its lines are so delicate, it almost seems to disappear.

CAFE SERIES, 1983

DESIGNER: Pelikan Design
COUNTRY: Denmark
STATUS: Mfr. by Fritz Hansen
Dist. by Rudd International
DIMENSIONS: Chair: W 20″
(50.8 cm), D 20¾″ (52.7 cm),
H 28″ (71.1 cm)

Here is another descendant of the Thonet B-9 Chair (page 13). The Café Series, crafted in the Danish tradition, includes the chair, a bar stool, and three tables. Their frames are made of tubular steel, with tabletops and seats also of steel. Chair seat and back are padded with gray rubber; tabletops are made of stainless steel left plain or lacquered gray, or of polished brass. The steel tubing is either galvanized or lacquered red, blue, or black.

LOUNGE CHAIR, 1980s

DESIGNER: Alexander
Ferdinand Porsche
COUNTRY: Germany
STATUS: Mfr. by Baker
Furniture Company;
Dist. by Baker, Knapp & Tubbs
DIMENSIONS: W 28½" (72.4 cm),
D 71" (180 cm), H 45"
(114 cm), AH 24" (61 cm)

Like the Porsche car, the chair is streamlined and sculptural; both appear to be in motion while at rest. The chair is adjustable from upright to reclining positions with several positions in between. Upholstered in calfskin suspended from a black ebonized aluminum frame, the Porsche Chair is exceptionally comfortable.

FORUM FURNITURE, 1980s

DESIGNERS: Stig Herman Olsen;
Per Kristian Dahl
COUNTRY: Denmark
STATUS: Mfr. by Ascan Form
DIMENSIONS: Variable

Forum Furniture proves that conference furniture can be versatile and practical as well as beautiful. This collection includes tables that can be combined with special assembly fittings in their corners. Table leafs can be added or microphones and lamps can be snap-fitted. Forum chairs are available with or without armrests; both can be stacked. The recess at the side of the seat allows the chairs to be attached into rows.

SYSTEM 25, 1980s

DESIGNER: Richard Sapper
(b. 1932)
COUNTRY: Germany
STYLE: Ergonomic
STATUS: Mfr. by Comforto
DIMENSIONS: W 22½" (57.2 cm),
D 17½" (44.5 cm), H 36"–40"
(91.5–101.5 cm)

Office productivity increases when the worker is comfortable, and comfort requires that seating be adjustable. System 25, created by the German designer Richard Sapper, has a patented mechanism and sectioned seat to allow the chair to move as the sitter moves. It supports as well in a reclining position as it does in an upright one. The chair can be obtained with a headrest as well as with a "memory return"—a computerized ability to remember the sitter's anatomical needs.

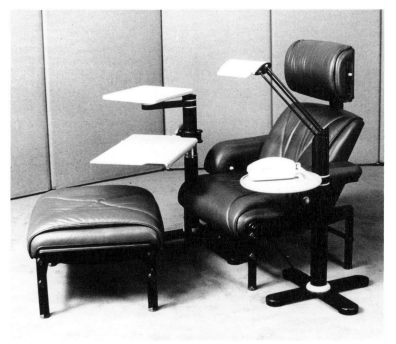

JEFFERSON CHAIR, 1985

DESIGNER: Niels Diffrient
(b. 1931)
COUNTRY: United States
STYLE: Ergonomic
STATUS: Mfr. by SunarHauserman
DIMENSIONS: W 34" (86.4 cm),
D 33" (83.8 cm), H 43" (109.2 cm)

Niels Diffrient is an industrial designer who approaches furniture design with an attitude similar to Bruno Mathsson's (page 98): His concerns are what he calls "pelvic cages," "spinal disks," pounds of "thrust." Although this chair is a tribute to Thomas Jefferson's well-conceived chaise planned for Monticello, his renowned home in Virginia, Diffrient's Jefferson Chair is no eighteenth-century design. Many adjustments of height and angles for back, seat, and arms are possible. Attachable accessories include stools, tables, and lights. Jefferson recalls the comfortable design of the Eames lounge (page 116).

ATLANTIS GROUP, 1982

DESIGNER: Wendell Castle
(b. 1932)
COUNTRY: United States
STYLE: Craft Revival
STATUS: Handcrafted;
Dist. by The Gunlocke Company
DIMENSIONS: Chair: W 29"
(73.7 cm), D 27" (68.5 cm),
H 30" (76.2 cm)

Atlantis is office furniture; the collection includes a desk, a credenza, and a chair. The pieces all have black-lacquered hardwood "coned" legs and bands topped with small gold-plated brass spheres. The feet of the legs are flattened spheres lacquered in turquoise, peach, or red. Wendell Castle's expert craftsmanship is evident in the details and finish of each piece. His work has been shown in major museums throughout the United States.

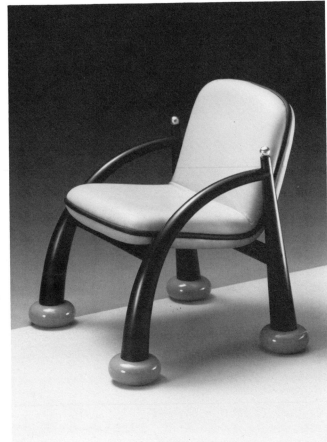

VENETIAN, 1983

DESIGNER: Stanley Jay
Friedman (b. 1939)
COUNTRY: United States
STYLE: Classical Modernism
STATUS: Mfr. by Bonaventure
Furniture Industries
DIMENSIONS: W 28½″ (72.3 cm),
D 37″ (94 cm), H 28″ (70 cm)

The Classical Modernism style evokes the International Style in its austerity and precision. The silhouettes may be different, but the plain unadorned look can be traced back to early modern principles. The collection to which this lounge belongs won the ASID Award and the IBD Award in 1983.

RUBBER CHAIR, 1983

DESIGNER: Brian Kane (b. 1948)
COUNTRY: United States
STATUS: Mfr. by Metropolitan
Furniture Corporation
DIMENSIONS: W 22″ (55.9 cm),
D 22″ (55.9 cm), H 30″ (76.2 cm),
AH 26″ (66 cm)

Winner of the IBD Silver Award in 1983 and the IDEA First Place Furniture Award in 1984, the Rubber Chair is considered one of Brian Kane's finest works. It is made of tubular steel. Its flexible back supports are encased in rubber tubing which is soft and resilient but tough enough for hard public use. It is easy to clean, and is stain- and burn-resistant. The maple seat comes in a natural or textured finish in several colors; an upholstered padded seat with a replaceable cover is also available.

ANDOVER ARMCHAIR, 1980s

DESIGNER: Davis Allen
COUNTRY: United States
STATUS: Mfr. by Stendig
International
DIMENSIONS: W 22″ (55.9 cm),
D 22½″ (57 cm), H 35″
(88.9 cm), SH 18″ (45.7 cm),
AH 26¼″ (67.3 cm)

Davis Allen is an associate of Skidmore, Owings, Merrill—the international architecture and design firm. Allen's Andover Chair has a solid beech frame available in several different finishes; the seat is foam on a webbed plywood frame upholstered with fabric, vinyl, or leather.

MEIER FURNITURE GROUP, 1982

DESIGNER: Richard Meier (b. 1934)
COUNTRY: United States
STATUS: Mfr. by Knoll International
DIMENSIONS: Chair: W 21″
(53.3 cm), D 20″ (50.8 cm),
H 27½″ (69.9 cm);
Chaise: W 72″ (182.9 cm), D 27½″
(69.9 cm), H 25⅛″ (63.8 cm)

Richard Meier is well known for his design of such buildings as High Museum in Atlanta, Georgia, and the Atheneum in New Harmony, Indiana. His architecture is strongly influenced by the International Style, but his furniture reflects the styles of Charles Rennie Mackintosh (pages 38–41) and Josef Hoffmann (pages 48–52). This group has a hard maple veneer and a solid maple frame available in black or white hand-rubbed finish.

ROCKING CHAIR, 1982

DESIGNER: Carlos Riart (b. 1944)
COUNTRY: Spain
STATUS: Mfr. by Knoll International
DIMENSIONS: W 24¾" (62.9 cm),
D 42½" (108 cm),
H 39¼" (99.5 cm)

Barcelona-based designer Carlos Riart was commissioned by Knoll International to design a chair to commemorate the Barcelona Exhibition of 1929. Made of ebony with Brazilian amaranth, the Rocking Chair has mother-of-pearl inlays or hollywood with ebony inlays in a simple design reminiscent of the International Style that Mies van der Rohe used for the German Pavilion at the Barcelona Exhibition. The seat and back of the chair are upholstered in a range of fabrics. It won the 1983 Roscoe Product Design Award.

TEATRO, 1982

DESIGNERS: Aldo Rossi; Luca Meda
COUNTRY: Italy
STATUS: Mfr. by Molteni
DIMENSIONS: W 18¹⁄₁₀" (46 cm),
D 19⁷⁄₁₀" (50 cm),
H 30³⁄₁₀" (77 cm)

Aldo Rossi's and Luca Meda's Teatro—designed to commemorate Teatro del Mondo, a floating theater—was the highlight of the 1980 Venice Biennale, an Italian design show. It was made of iron tubes clad with pine, welded at its base to a barge, and launched into a Venetian canal. The Teatro has a lacquered wood frame with an upholstered seat and back.

TORSO, 1982

DESIGNER: Archizoom/
Paolo Deganello
COUNTRY: Italy
STATUS: Mfr. by Cassina
Dist. by Atelier International
DIMENSIONS: W 57″ (144.8 cm),
D 43″ (109.2 cm),
H 45¾″ (116.2 cm)

In 1982 Paolo Deganello of Archizoom, the Florence-based team of architects and designers, designed the Torso for Cassina. The collection, which includes sofas, armchairs, and a bed, are made with steel structures, elastic webbing, and padded upholstery in leather or fabric. The seat and back of a chair or sofa may have different upholstery material and/or different colors. Attachable round tables in gray, black, or ochre lacquered wood are available for the highback sofa and asymmetrical chairs. The design owes a great deal to the designs of the 1950s.

ARMCHAIR, 1982

DESIGNER: Michael Graves
(b. 1934)
COUNTRY: United States
STYLE: Post-Modern
STATUS: Mfr. by SunarHauserman
DIMENSIONS: W 32″ (81.2 cm),
D 29″ (73.7 cm), H 28¾″ (73 cm)

Architect Michael Graves has designed some of the world's most controversial structures, including the Humana Building in Louisville, Kentucky, and the Portland Building in Oregon. His distinctive style is influenced by motifs from the classical past; he has rejected the rules of modern architecture as set down by the Bauhaus. This armchair shows the influence of the Art Deco period. The frame is bird's-eye maple veneer with an upholstered seat and back. Graves is also known for his work with the Memphis design group (pages 182–183).

ECLIPSE CHAIR, 1985

DESIGNER: Jay Spectre
COUNTRY: United States
STYLE: Post-Modern
STATUS: Mfr. by Century Furniture
DIMENSIONS: W 26½" (67.3 cm),
D 35" (89 cm), H 33½" (85 cm),
SH 17½" (44.5 cm),
AH 24½" (62.2 cm)

The Eclipse Chair is considered the signature piece of the collection designed for Century by Jay Spectre, one of America's most prominent interior designers. Bleached white oak arches form the back legs and arms and straight polished columns of metal form the front legs. The upholstery, in fabric of Spectre's own design, is sewn into horizontal channels. The Eclipse won top honors at the Southern Furniture Market in High Point, North Carolina.

DE MENIL TABLE, 1983

DESIGNERS: Gwathmey Siegel/
Robert Siegel (b. 1939);
Charles Gwathmey (b. 1938)
COUNTRY: United States
STATUS: Mfr. by ICF
DIMENSIONS: H 18" (45.7 cm),
Top is variable

The top of this table by Gwathmey Siegel is made of solid wood and wood veneer in cherry, mahogany, walnut, ebonized elm, natural or rosewood-stained ash. Brass insets are available too. The tabletop on this table is 1½" thick; the dining table is 2¼" thick. They are both available in square, rectangular, and round models. Base, top, and top border are made with contrasting woods; the excellent craftsmanship is obvious.

GRANDE FLUTE, 1985

DESIGNER: Angelo Donghia
(1935–1985)
COUNTRY: United States
STYLE: Classic Modern
STATUS: Mfr. by Donghia Furniture
DIMENSIONS: W 28½" (72.4 cm),
D 29" (73.7 cm), H 38½" (97.8 cm)

With the design of the Grande Flute in 1985, Angelo Donghia brought Louis XVI into the late twentieth century. Generously scaled, the Grande Flute has deeply cut fluting on the frames and legs, highlighting the classic lines of the piece. The Flute, designed by Donghia in 1984, is similar but smaller. Both are available in gold leaf, silver leaf, pickled oak, and red or brown ebonized mahogany finish on oak.

STEAMER COLLECTION, 1982

DESIGNER: Thomas Lamb
COUNTRY: Canada
STATUS: Mfr. by Ambiant
Systems Ltd.
DIMENSIONS: Chair W 24" (61 cm),
D 35" (88.9 cm), H 34"
(86.4 cm), SH 11" (27.9 cm)

The Steamer Collection was created by prominent Canadian industrial designer Thomas Lamb. Included in The Museum of Modern Art's Permanent Collection, it won the 1982 Roscoe Award and the 1983 Product Design Gold Award. These chairs have wood veneers of Canadian maple lacquered clear or black. Their undulating curves and strip design renew a traditional silhouette. Coordinating tables feature glass slab tabletops.

BODYFORM CHAIR, 1980

DESIGNER: Peter Danko (b. 1949)
COUNTRY: United States
STATUS: Mfr. by Peter Danko
& Associates
DIMENSIONS: W 20½" (52 cm),
D 22" (56 cm), H 30" (76.2 cm)

Peter Danko has been instrumental in exploiting the full potential of bent plywood design pioneered earlier by Charles and Ray Eames, Alvar Aalto, and Gerald Summers. Molded out of one sheet of plywood, Bodyform is produced by a robot. The chair is in the Permanent Collection of The Museum of Modern Art in New York City.

SERIE EDO, 1981

DESIGNER: Kisho Kurokawa
(b. 1934)
COUNTRY: Japan
STATUS: Mfr. by Kosuga & Company

Kisho Kurokawa was one of the first Japanese architects to break with the modern tradition. His technically advanced Nakagin Capsule Building in Tokyo and his Sony Tower in Osaka are representative of his work. His furniture is also innovative. This Serie Edo Chair has a flowing high back made of ebonized wood lacquered purple. The seat is leather. The collection also includes a coffee table, small and large dining tables, and an armchair.

CARLTON, 1981

DESIGNER: Ettore Sottsass Jr.
(b. 1917)
COUNTRY: Austria/Italy
STYLE: Memphis
STATUS: Mfr. by Memphis Milano
DIMENSIONS: W 74¾" (190 cm),
D 15½" (40 cm), H 77" (196 cm)

The name Memphis was taken from the Bob Dylan song, "Stuck Outside of Mobile with the Memphis Blues Again," by a design group that caused a sensation when they first ex-hibited at the 1981 Milan Furniture Fair. Austrian-born Ettore Sottsass Jr., is the founder and father of this group of 20 who create furnishings from odd, brilliant colors and shapes with humor and style. The Carlton is a room divider with bookshelves incorporating slabs, boxes, two drawers, and projecting members. Each wood component is covered with plastic laminate in red, purple, green, yellow, gray, white, black, or brown.

ZABRO CHAISE RONDE, 1980s

DESIGNERS: Studio Alchymia/
Alessandro Mendini; Bruno Gregori
COUNTRY: Italy
STATUS: Mfr. by Zabro

In 1976, Studio Alchymia, a collaboration of designers and a manufacturer, was founded. And then in 1984, Zabro, a factory, was set up to produce the Nuova Alchymia collection. This painted furniture combined traditional craft techniques with high-tech materials and processes. The Chaise Ronde is a chair that can be changed into a table by tilting the circular back. When the round form is upright, the painted back section and seat create a colorful abstract composition.

LORRY, 1984

DESIGNER: Thomas Lear Grace
COUNTRY: United States
STYLE: Memphis
STATUS: Mfr. by Grace Designs
DIMENSIONS: W 17" (42.8 cm),
H 35½" (90.1 cm)

Thomas Lear Grace named this chair for his partner, Lorry Park. The base is made of a black square, which, like the seat, is made of maple. The back seat bands are made of birch. Lorry comes in a natural finish or in combinations of three colors. The idea was to capture a psychological moment; Grace Designs wanted to foster new ideas and concepts in furniture.

ROYAL, 1983

DESIGNER: Nathalie du Pasquier
COUNTRY: France
STYLE: Memphis
STATUS: Mfr. by Memphis Milano
DIMENSIONS: W 78¾" (200 cm),
D 29½" (75 cm), H 37½" (95 cm)

One of the most universally admired pieces to come out of the Memphis group is the Royal Chaise by the French textile designer Nathalie du Pasquier. The Royal Chaise has a plastic laminated frame and cotton cushions. Cushions and frame are printed with three compatible but contrasting abstract patterns in red, green, purple, and blue.

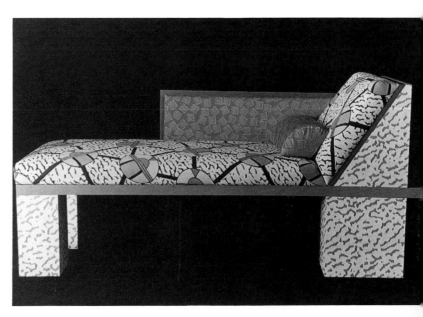

PRISMA, 1984

DESIGNER: Milo Baughman
(b. 1923)
COUNTRY: United States
STYLE: Memphis
STATUS: Not in production

Prisma was designed by Milo Baughman and produced by Thayer Coggin in bright colors and simple shapes. Chairs and sofas came in blue, orange, yellow, black, and mauve; bases were upholstered in the same wool fabric over hardwood frames, in contrasting colors, or, for some pieces, in brass or chrome. The humor and playfulness characteristic of the Memphis style is well displayed in this colorful collection.

QUEEN ANNE, QUEEN ANNE, 1981

DESIGNERS: Terence (b. 1954) and
Laura (b. 1953) Main
COUNTRY: United States
STYLE: Art Furniture
STATUS: Collection, Art et Industrie
DIMENSIONS: W 24" (61 cm),
H 45" (114.3 cm),
D 24" (61 cm)

This chair gives the impression of a doubly exposed photograph. The husband-and-wife design team of Terence and Laura Main wanted to wake up the beholder. Their work is playful and sophisticated. Here they bring in a style from the past and color it red and yellow.

NOTHING CONTINUES TO HAPPEN, 1981

DESIGNER: Howard Meister
(b. 1953)
COUNTRY: United States
STYLE: Art Furniture
STATUS: Collection, Art et Industrie
DIMENSIONS: W 37" (94 cm),
D 16" (40.6 cm),
H 17" (42.8 cm)

Some unique furniture models for the 1980s were created by artists. Nothing Continues to Happen, created by folk artist Howard Meister, emerged as an icon of this new direction. The function as a chair is recognizable but Meister has also expressed his view of the current world condition.

VENTURI COLLECTION, 1980s

DESIGNER: Robert Venturi (b. 1925)
COUNTRY: United States
STYLE: Post-Modern
STATUS: Mfr. by Knoll International
DIMENSIONS: Variable

Philadelphia architect Robert Venturi's furniture is reminiscent of styles from the past while being very much the latest thing. The chairs he has done for Knoll International include the Empire, the Hepplewhite, the Sheraton, the Chippendale, and the Art Deco. Chippendale, with its Grandma's Print upholstery, was shown in 1985 at the Whitney Museum of American Art's High Styles: Twentieth Century American Design show in New York City.

MANHATTAN SUITE, 1980s

DESIGNER: Frank Siciliano (b. 1946)
STYLE: Art Furniture
COUNTRY: United States
STATUS: Handcrafted
DIMENSIONS: H 5'–6'3"
(152.4–190.5 cm)

Artist and set designer Frank Siciliano has created 10 distinctive conference chairs inspired by well-known New York City architecture. The soaring chairs have column legs and are constructed of solid cherrywood. Siciliano hand paints each chair with automobile metallic lacquer to define the building's details. Each chair in the Manhattan Suite collection weighs about 150 pounds.

TRAMONTO A NEW YORK, 1980

DESIGNER: Gaetano Pesce
COUNTRY: Italy
STATUS: Mfr. by Cassina
DIMENSIONS: W 87¾″ (222.9 cm),
D 40¾″ (103.5 cm),
H 46¾″ (118.7 cm)

Gaetano Pesce was a founding member of Group N in Padua. Since 1962 he has worked as an interior designer in Paris, New York, and Venice. This three-seat sofa has a plywood frame and foam polyurethane and polyester padding. Its upholstery is meant to suggest windows on buildings. Tramonto a New York is part of the Permanent Collection of The Museum of Modern Art in New York City.

KIPS BAY SOFA, 1980s

DESIGNER: John F. Saladino
COUNTRY: United States
STATUS: Mfr. by Dunbar
DIMENSIONS: W 60″
(152.4 cm), D 36″ (91.4 cm),
H 26″ (66 cm)

Based in New York since 1972, John Saladino is considered one of the nation's top interior designers. He is known for borrowing styles from the past and injecting them with new life. The Kips Bay Sofa has a gathered fabric covered base, a long backrest pillow, and a loose-pleated seat cover. It is typical of his sophisticated and elegant style.

VERANDA, 1983

DESIGNER: Vico Magistretti
COUNTRY: Italy
STATUS: Mfr. by Cassina;
Dist. by Atelier International
DIMENSIONS: W 37⅘″
(96 cm), D 33½″
(85.1 cm), H 29½–43³⁄₁₀″
(74.9–110 cm)

Veranda can be opened wide to be a lounge chair or be closed into an armchair. The armchair has a frame made of folding steel with a glossy dark green or mat-black enamelled steel base. Veranda is included in the Permanent Collection of The Museum of Modern Art in New York City.

WINK LOUNGE CHAIR, 1980

DESIGNER: Toshiyuki Kita (b. 1942)
COUNTRY: Japan
STATUS: Mfr. by Cassina;
Dist. by Atelier International
DIMENSIONS: D 35½″ (90.1 cm),
W 30¾″ (77.5 cm), H 37–31½″
(94–80 cm), SH 15″ (38.1 cm),
L 78¾″ (200 cm)

In 1964, after studying at the University of Design in Osaka, Toshiyuki Kita opened his own firm there. Since then he has received many design honors and awards. His Wink Chair is part of the Permanent Collection of The Museum of Modern Art in New York City. Fully adjustable, Wink has a steel frame with attached foam polyurethane and polyester padding upholstered in colorful zipper-fastened fabrics or leather. The unusual headrest is divided into two parts, each with an independent reclining mechanism.

DIRECTORIES

AMBIANT SYSTEMS LTD.
76 Richmond Street East
M5C 1P1 Toronto
Canada

Thomas Lamb   Steamer Collection

AB KARL ANDERSSON & SÖNER
Box 173
56122 Huskvarna
Sweden

Borge Morgensen   Asserbo Chair 504

ARCONOS CORPORATION
580 Orwell Street
Mississauga, Ontario L5A 3V7
Canada

Olivier Mourgue   Bouloum

ARFLEX S.p.A.
Via Monte Rosa, 27
20051 Limbiate (Milano)
Italy

Franco Albini   Fiorenza

ARKITEKTURA
Corporate Headquarters
P.O. Box 210
Princeton, N.J. 08540

Eliel Saarinen   Side Chair

ARTEK
Keskuskatu 3
00100 Helsinki 10
Finland
Distributor in U.S.A.: ICF, Inc.

Alvar Aalto   Paimio Chair (410); Stools
and Tables; Tea Trolley; Pension
Armchair (406); Armchair

ARTEMIDE
Via Burghiera
2000 Pregnanna Milanese
Milan
Italy
Distributor in U.S.A.:
Artemide
150 East 58th Street, New York, N.Y. 10155

Vico Magistretti   Gaudi Chair; Selene
Stacking Chair

ARTIFORT
Wagemans Maastricht BV
6214 AA Maastricht
St. Annalaan 23
The Netherlands
Distributor in U.S.A.: Krueger

Geoffrey Harcourt   Chair 506
Pierre Paulin   Ribbon Chair 582;
Chair 300; Chair 577

ASCAN FORM
Gjellerupvej 84
DK-8230 Abyhoj
Denmark

Stig H. Olsen, Per K. Dahl   Forum Furniture

ASKO OY
Postiosoite
PL/Box 45
SF-15101 Lahti 10
Finland

Eero Aarnio   Globe; Mushroom; Gyro

ATELIER INTERNATIONAL, LTD.
235 Express Street
Plainview, N.Y. 11803
*Distributor and manufacturer under license
from Cassina S.p.A.*

Erik Gunnar Asplund   Goteborg I;
Goteborg II; Senna Chair
Mario Bellini   Cab Chair
Paolo Deganello   Torso
Toshiyuki Kita   Wink
Le Corbusier   Basculant (LC-1) Chair;
LC-2 (Petit Confort): LC-4 (Pony)
Chaise; LC-7 (Siege Tournant)
Armchair
Charles Rennie Mackintosh   Argyle
Chair; Argyle Armchair; Hill House I;
Willow I; D. S. Collection
Vico Magistretti   Maralunga; Veranda
Gerrit Rietveld   Red/Blue Chair; Shröder
Table; Zigzag Chair; Crate Furniture
Tobia and Afra Scarpa   Soriana Group,
Chair 925
Frank Lloyd Wright   Robie Chairs; Allen
Table; Midway Chair; Barrel Chair

AVARTE OY
Kalenvankatu 16, SF-00100
Helsinki
Finland

Yrjo Kukkapuro   Karuselli

B & B ITALIA S.p.A.
22060 Novedrate (Como)
Strada Provinciale
Italy

Gaetano Pesce   Series Up

B.D. EDICIONES DE DISEÑO
Mallorca 291
08037 Barcelona 37
Spain
*Distributor in U.SA.: Furniture of the
Twentieth Century*

Antoni Gaudi   Calvet Chair
Charles Rennie Mackintosh   Hill House
Chair; Ingram Street Chair

BAKER FURNITURE COMPANY
Department 352
1661 Monroe Avenue
Grand Rapids, Mich. 49505
Distributor in U.S.A.:
Baker, Knapp & Tubbs
200 Lexington Avenue
New York, N.Y. 10016

Alexander Ferdinand Porsche   Porsche Chair

BARESEL-BOFINGER
Gutenbergstr. 39
D-7100 Heilbronn
West Germany

Hans Gugelot   M125 Modular Group

BELLATO S.p.A.
(Elco Bellato S.p.A.)
30037 Scorze (Ve)
Via Treviso 99
Italy

Cesare Leonardi, Franca Stagi   Dondola

BONAVENTURE FURNITURE INDUSTRIES
894 Bloomfield
Montreal, H2V 356
Canada

Stanley Jay Friedman   Venetian

BOTIUM
Bella Center, Central Boulevard
2300 Kobenhavn S
Denmark

Rud Thygesen, Johnny Sorensen   Royal
Furniture

BRICKEL ASSOCIATES
515 Madison Avenue
New York, N.Y. 10022

Ward Bennett   University Chair

BROWN JORDAN
9860 Gidley Street
P.O. Box 5688
El Monte, Calif. 91734

Tadao E. Inouye   Kantan Collection

CASSINA S.p.A.
Via Luigi Busnelli 1
20036 Meda
Milan
Italy
Distributor in U.S.A.: Atelier
International Ltd.

Erik Gunnar Asplund   Senna Chair;
Goteborg I; Goteborg II
Mario Bellini   IL Colonnato Tables; Cab
Chair; Chair 932/2
Paolo Deganello   AEO; Torso
Gianfranco Frattini   Modello 780
Toshiyuki Kita   Wink
Le Corbusier   Basculant (LC-1) Chair;
LC-2 (Petit Confort); LC-4 (Pony)
Chaise; LC-7 (Siege Tournant) Armchair
Charles Rennie Mackintosh   Argyle
Chair; Argyle Armchair; Hill House I;
Willow I; D.S. Collection
Vico Magistretti   Maralunga; Veranda
Gaetano Pesce   Series Sit-Down;
Tramonto a New York
Gio Ponti   Superleggera
Gerrit Rietveld   Red/Blue Chair; Zigzag
Chair; Schröder Table; Crate Furniture
Tobia and Afra Scarpa   Soriana Group;
Chair 925
Frank Lloyd Wright   Robie Chairs; Allen
Table; Midway Chair; Barrel Chair

WENDELL CASTLE INC.
18 Maple Street
Scottsville, N.Y. 14546
Distributor: The Gunlocke Company

Wendell Castle   Atlantis Group

CENTURY FURNITURE COMPANY
P.O. Box 608
Hickory, N.C. 28603

Jay Spectre   Eclipse Chair

CITTERIO S.p.A.
Societa per azioni
22040 Sirone (Como)
Via Provinciale 16
Italy

Joseph Beverly Fenby   Tripolina Chair

COMFORT, GEORGETTI FRATELLI & CO./
STUDIO JOE COLOMBO
Via Seveso 19
20036 Meda (Milano)
Italy

Joe Colombo   Elda Chair

COMFORTO INCORPORATED
P.O. Box 917
Lincolnton, N.C. 28092

Richard Sapper   System 25

PETER DANKO & ASSOCIATES INC.
7492 F Old Alexander Ferry Road
Clinton, Md. 20735

Peter Danko   Bodyform Chair

D.S.I.
(Design Selections International, Inc.)
150 East 58th Street
New York, N.Y. 10155
Distributor for Fritz Hansen and Carl
Hansen and Son

Hans Wegner   Chair (24); Peacock Chair
(JH 550); "The" Chair

DELTA EXPORT
(see Nikol Internazionale/Delta Export)

DONGHIA FURNITURE COMPANY, LTD.
41 East 11th Street
New York, N.Y. 10014

Angelo Donghia   Grande Flute

DUNBAR
601 South Fulton Street
Berne, Ind. 46711

John Saladino   Kips Bay Sofa

DUX INTERNATIONAL MÖBEL AB
S-231 00 Trelleborg
Sweden
Distributor in U.S.A.:
Dux Interiors, Inc.
305 East 63rd Street
New York, N.Y. 10021

Bruno Mathsson   Lounge

ELCO BALLATO S.p.A. (see Bellato S.p.A.)

ESCART INTERNATIONAL
6, Rue Ravee
75004 Paris
France
Distributor in U.S.A.: Furniture of the
Twentieth Century

Eileen Gray   Transat Chair
Robert Mallet-Stevens   Chair

formes nouvelles
22 Boulevard Raspail
75007 Paris
France
Distributor in U.S.A: J. G. Furniture
Systems Inc.

René Herbst   Reclining Lounge Chair

FURNITURE OF THE TWENTIETH CENTURY
227 West 17th Street
New York, N.Y. 10011
Distributor for Ecart International, B.D.
Ediciones de Diseño, and Windmill

Marcel Breuer   Isokon Lounge
Eileen Gray   Transat Chair
Charles Rennie Mackintosh   Hill House
Chair; Ingram Chair

Robert Mallet-Stevens   Chair
Giuseppe Terragni   Monza Armchair

GF FURNITURE SYSTEMS
P.O. Box 1108
Youngstown, Ohio 44501

David Rowland   GF 40/4 Chair

GIOVANNETTI
Casella Postale 1
51032 Bottegone (Pistoia)
Italy

Alessandro Becchi   Anfibio Sofa

GRACE DESIGNS
World Trade Center #622
P.O. Box 58108
Dallas, Tex. 75258
Distributor for Memphis Milano

Thomas Lear Grace   Lorry Chair

GRETCHEN BELLINGER INC.
330 East 59th Street
New York, N.Y. 10022

T. H. Robsjohn-Gibbings   Klismos Chair

GUFRAM
S.n.c. Industria arredamento
Via Tanseschie, 14
10073 Cirie (Torino)
Italy

Piero Gilardi   Sassi (Rocks)
Studio 65   Ionic

THE GUNLOCKE COMPANY
One Gunlocke Drive
Wayland, N.Y. 14572
Distributor for Wendell Castle, Inc.

Wendell Castle   Atlantis Group

CARL HANSEN AND SON A/S
Kochsgade 97
Odense
Denmark
Distributor in U.S.A.: DSI

Hans Wegner   Chair 24

FRITZ HANSEN eft, A/S
DK-3450, Allerod
Denmark
Distributor in U.S.A.: Rudd International
Corp.

Arne Jacobsen   Oxford Collection;
Swan and Egg
Poul Kjaerholm   Chair 22; Armchair 11;
Hammock Chair 24; Chair 20
Henning Larsen   Chair
Verner Panton   Panton System 1–2–3
Pelikan Design   Café Series
Hans Wegner   China Chair

JOHANNES HANSENS MØBELSKEDKERI
Bredgade 65
Kobenhaven K
Denmark
Distributor in U.S.A.: DSI

Hans Wegner   Peacock Chair, "The" Chair

HILLE INTERNATIONAL LTD.
365 Euston Road
London NW1 3AR
U.K.
North American manufacturer under license
from Hille and Source One

Robin Day   Polyprop Chair

ICF, Inc.
305 East 63rd Street
New York, N.Y. 10021

Alvar Aalto   Paimio Chair (41); Pension
Armchair (406); Tea Trolley; Stools and
Tables
Alessandro Becchi   Anfibio Sofa
Giandomenico Belotti   Spaghetti Chair
Mario Botta   87 Seconda Armchair
Marcel Breuer   Lounge
Archille Castiglioni   Mezzadro Tractor
Seating; Primate Kneeling Stool
Gatti, Paolini, Teodoro   Sacco
Gwathmey Siegel   deMenil Table
Niels Jorgen Haugesen   Network Stacking
System
Josef Hoffmann   Purkersdorf Chair;
Fledermaus Chair; Armlöffel Chair;
Kubus Chair; Haus Koller Chair; Two-Seat
Sofa; Rocking Chair; Palais Stoclet Chair

Gabriele Mucchi Genni Lounge
Eliel Saarinen White Collection; Blue Collection
Philippe Starck Café Costes Chairs; Dr. Sonderbar; Richard III

ICF, ITALY
280 Strada Padano Superiore
2090 Vimodrone
Milano
Italy

Katavolos, Littell, Kelley T-Chair

J.G. FURNITURE SYSTEMS INC.
121 Park Avenue
Quakertown, Pa. 18951
Distributor in U.S.A. for formes nouvelles

René Herbst Reclining Lounge Chair

KARTELL
Via delle Industrie
20082 Noveglio (Milano)
Italy
Distributor in U.S.A.:
Kartell, U.S.A.
Liberty Highway, Easley, S.C. 29640

Joe Colombo Chair 4860
Anna Castelli Ferrieri Stacking Storage Thing
Marco Zanuso, Richard Saper Small Child's Chair

KNOLL INTERNATIONAL
The Knoll Building
655 Madison Avenue
New York, N.Y. 10021

Gae Aulenti Aulenti Collection
Harry Bertoia Highback Chair
Cini Boeri Lunario Table
Richard Meier Meier Furniture Group
Ludwig Mies van der Rohe MR Chair; MR Lounges; Barcelona Group; Brno Armchair; Tugendhat Chair
Warren Platner Wire Collection
Charles Pollock Swivel Armchair
Carlos Riart Rocking Chair
Eero Saarinen Womb Chair; Tulip Pedestal Group

Tobia Scarpa Bastiano Group
Richard Schultz Leisure Collection
Kazuhide Takahaa Suzanne Lounge
Robert Venturi Venturi Collection

KOSUGA & CO., LTD.
15-4 2-chome, Higashi-Nikonbashi
Chuo-ku, Tokyo
Japan

Kisho Kurokawa Serie Edo

KROIN INC.
Charles Square, Suite 300
Cambridge, Mass. 02138

Heinz Wirth Offenburg Park Chair

KRÜEGER FURNITURE
116 Wilbur Place
P.O. Box 509
Bohemia, N.Y. 11716
Distributor for Artifort

Geoffrey Harcourt Chair 506
Pierre Paulin Ribbon Chair 582; Chair 300; Chair 577
Giancarlo Piretti Plia Chair

JACK LENOR LARSEN
41 East 11th Street
New York, N.Y. 10003

Richard Riemerschmid Oak Side Chair

THE McGUIRE COMPANY
1201 Bryant Street
San Francisco, Calif. 94103

Elenor Forbes Rattan OH-9 Officers' Chair
Elinor McGuire Willow (W-5) Chair

JUDY KENSLEY McKIE
462 Putnam Avenue
Cambridge, Mass. 02139

Judy Kensley McKie Bench with Horses

JOHN MAKEPEACE DESIGNERS
Parnham House
Dorset
U.K.

John Makepeace Ebony Gothic Chair

SAM MALOOF STUDIO
P.O. Box 51
Alta Loma, Calif.

Sam Maloof Rocking Chair

JOHN MASCHERONI DESIGNS
200 East 64th Street
New York, N.Y. 10021

John Mascheroni Chair 424; Tubo Table

MEMPHIS MILANO/ETTORE SOTTSASS JR.
19 via Pontaccio
10121 Milano
Italy

Nathalie du Pasquier Royal
Ettore Sottsass Jr. Carlton

METROPOLIAN FURNITURE CORPORATION
245 East Harris Avenue
South San Francisco, Calif. 94080

Brian Kane Rubber Chair

MEWA P. + W. BLATTMANN
Metallwarenfabrik AG
Zuger Strasse 64 8820
Wadenswil
Switzerland

Hans Coray Landi Stacking Chair

HERMAN MILLER, INC.
8500 Bryon Road
Zeeland, Mich. 49464

Don Chadwick Chadwick Modular Seating
Charles and Ray Eames LCM Dining Chair; DCW Molded Plywood Chair; DAR Shell Chair; DKR Shell Chair; Lounge Chair 670; Chaise; Aluminum Group Chair; Tandem Sling Seating
George Nelson Sling Sofa
Isamu Noguchi IN50 Table
Robert Propst Action Office System

NIENKÄMPER
415 Finchdene Square
Scarborough, Ontario M1X 1B7
Canada

Verner Panton Panton Stacking Chair

DIRECTORIES

NIKOL INTERNAZIONALE/DELTA EXPORT
Via Cavalleggeri de Saluzzo 2
33097 Spilimbergo (PN)
Italy

Vladimir Tatlin   Chair

OCA
Rio de Janeiro
Brazil

Sergio Rodriguez   Sherriff Chair

OLIVETTI SYNTHESIS S.p.A.
Largo Richini 6
20122 Milano
Italy

Ettore Sottsass Jr.   Typing Chair Z9/r

PLYCRAFT INC.
39 South Canal Street
P.O. Box 1229
Lawrence, Mass. 01842

Paul Goldman   Rockwell Chair

POLTRONOVA, PISTOIA
Arredamenti s.r.l., 1-51031
Agliana (Pistoia)
Italy

Studio Design   Joe Lounge Chair

HARVEY PROBBER INC.
315 East 62nd Street
New York, N.Y. 10021

Harvey Probber   Armchair 8043

RUDD INTERNATIONAL CORPORATION
1025 Thomas Jefferson Street NW
Washington, D.C. 20007
Distributor for Fritz Hansen

Arne Jacobsen   Swan and Egg; Ant
(Series 7); Oxford Collection
Poul Kjaerholm   Chair 22; Armchair 11;
Armchair 12; Hammock Chair 24;
Chair 20
Henning Larsen   Chair
Verner Panton   Panton System 1–2–3
Pelikan Design   Café Series
Hans Wegner   China Chair

RUD. RASMUSSENS SNEDKERIER APS
Norregrogade 45
DK 2200 Kobenhavn
Denmark

Kaare Klint   Safari Chair; Deck Chair
Mogens Koch   MK Safari Chair

SCANFORM (See Ascan Form)

SKIPPER S.p.A (Skipper/Arcani)
Via Serbelloni 1
20122 Milano
Italy

Angelo Mangiarotti   3 Tre Chair

SORMANI S.p.A.
Via M. Madalena, 37
22060 Arosio (Como)
Italy

Joe Colombo   Additional System Lounge
Claudio Sallocchi   Appoggio Chair

SOURCE ONE
646 Magnetic Drive
Downsview, Ontario M35 2C4
Canada

Robin Day   Polyprop Chair

STENDIG INTERNATIONAL
140 East 62nd Street
New York, N.Y. 10021

Davis Allen   Andover Chair
Marcel Breuer   Cesca Chair
Eileen Gray   Smoking Table
Josef Hoffmann   Prague Chair
Yrjo Kukkapuro   Karuselli
Eleanora Peduzzi-Riva   Nonstop Sofa
Studio 65   Marilyn

STOW & DAVIS
25 Summer Avenue NW
P.O. Box 2608
Grand Rapids, Mich. 49501

Robert De Fuccio   Triangle Chair

JOHN STUART INTERNATIONAL
(See Source One)

STUDIO FRANK SICILIANO
110 West 26th Street
New York, N.Y. 10001

Frank Siciliano   Manhattan Suite

SUNARHAUSERMAN
18 Marshall Street
Norwalk, Conn. 06854

Niels Diffrient   Jefferson Chair
Michael Graves   Armchair

THONET INDUSTRIES
491 East Princess Street
P.O. Box 1587
York, Pa. 17405

Marcel Breuer   Cesca Chair; Wassily
Chair; Lounge
Joan Burgasser   Club Tub
Josef Hoffmann   Prague Chair;
Fledermaus Chair
Anton Lorenz   Armchair
David Rowland   Sof-Tech
Michael Thonet   Bentwood Rocker;
Chair No. 14; Corbusier Chair

NIELS VODDER
Bille Brahesvej 2
Kobenhavn
Denmark

Finn Juhl   Easy Chair

WINDMILL FURNITURE
Turnham Green Terrace Mews
Chiswick, London W4 IQU
U.K.
*Distributor in U.S.A.: Furniture of the
Twentieth Century*

Marcel Breuer   Isokon Lounge Chair

FRANZ WITTMAN
A-3492, Etsdorf Am Kamp
Austria
Manufacturer in U.S.A.: ICF, Inc.

Josef Hoffmann   Rocking Chair; Kubus
Chair; Armlöffel Chair; Fledermaus
Chair; Haus Koller Chair; Two-Seat Sofa
Koloman Moser   Purkersdorf Chair

ZABRO OF MILAN
Studio Alchymia
Milano
Italy

Zabro of Milan   Zabro Chaise Ronde

ZANOTTA S.p.A.
Via Vittorio Veneto 57
20054 Nova Milanese (Milano)
Italy
Distributors in U.S.A.: ICF, Inc. and Furniture of the Twentieth Century

Gae Aulenti   Solus
DePas, D'Urbino, Lomazzi   Blow Chair
Design Studio   Sacco
Giuseppe Terragni   Monza Armchair

MUSEUMS AND GALLERIES

ART ET INDUSTRIE
594 Broadway
New York, N.Y. 10012

Terrence and Laura Main   Queen Anne, Queen Anne
Howard Meister   Nothing Continues to Happen

THE ART INSTITUTE OF CHICAGO
Michigan Avenue at Adams Street
Chicago, Ill. 60603

George Grant Elmslie   Chair
George Washington Maher   Library Table

COOPER-HEWITT MUSEUM
The Smithsonian Institution's National Museum of Design
1 East 91st Street
New York, N.Y. 10128

Frank Lloyd Wright   Chair for the Imperial Hotel

DANSKE KUNSTINDUSTRIMUSEET
Bregade 68
1260 Copenhagen
Denmark

Georges de Feure   Sofa for the Paris Exposition

FRANK LLOYD WRIGHT HOME AND STUDIO FOUNDATION
951 Chicago Avenue
Oak Park, Ill. 60302

Frank Lloyd Wright   Dining Chairs

50/FIFTY
793 Broadway
New York, N.Y. 10003

Norman Cherner   Chair

BARRY FRIEDMAN LTD., NEW YORK
243 East 82nd Street
New York, N.Y. 10028

Carlo Bugatti   Armchair
Victor Horta   Side Chair
Louis Majorelle   Armchair
Bruno Mathsson   Lounge
Gerald Summers   Bent Plywood Chair
Otto Wagner   Postal Savings Bank Chair

GAMBLE HOUSE
4 Westmoreland Place
Pasadena, Calif. 91103

Charles and Henry Greene   Armchair

GEMEENTEMUSEUM
The Hague
The Netherlands

Hendrikus Petrus Berlage   Oak Buffett

GRAND RAPIDS ART MUSEUM
155 Division North
Grand Rapids, Mich. 49503

Paul Frankl   Combination Desk and Bookcase

JORDAN-VOLPE GALLERY
457 West Broadway
New York, N.Y. 10012

Harvey Ellis   Armchair
Elbert Hubbard   Roycrofter Furniture
Gustav Stickley   Side Chair and Shirtwaist Box

KUNSTGEWERBEMUSEUM
c/o Staaliche Museen Kulturbesitz
1000 Berlin 61
West Germany

Bernhard Pankok   Vitrine

THE METROPOLITAN MUSEUM OF ART
5th Avenue at 82nd Street
New York, N.Y. 10028

Jules-Emile Leleu   Cabinet
Jacques-Emile Ruhlmann   Desk and File

MUSÉE DES ARTS DÉCORATIFS, THE LOUVRE
Rue de Rivoli
Paris
France

Emile Gallé   Chair
Hector Guimard   Chair
Paul Iribe   Armchair
Pierre Legrain   Chaise Lounge
Clement Rousseau   Sunburst Chair
Jacques-Emile Ruhlmann   Cabinet

MUSEUM FÜR KUNST UND GERWERBE, HAMBURG
Steintorplatz - D-2000
Hamburg 1
West Germany

Akseli Gallén-Kallela   Chair

MUSEUM OF FINE ARTS, BOSTON
465 Huntington Avenue
Boston, Mass. 02115

Judy Kensley McKie   Bench with Horses
Henry Hobson Richardson   Cathedral Chair

THE MUSEUM OF MODERN ART
11 West 53rd Street
New York, N.Y. 10019

Sir Isaac Cole   Bentwood Chair
Marcel Breuer   Armchair
Hector Guimard   Desk
Frank Lloyd Wright   Office Armchairs

NORDENFJELDSKE KUNSTINDUSTRIMUSEUM
Post: Munkegaten 5
7000 Trondheim
Norway

Henri van de Velde   Armchair

DIRECTORIES

PHILADELPHIA MUSEUM OF ART
Benjamin Franklin Parkway
Box 7646
Philadelphia, Pa. 19101

Joe Colombo   Chair 4860

MAX PROTETCH GALLERY
37 West 57th Street
New York, N.Y. 10019

Scott Burton   Aluminum Chair

STAATLICHE MUSEUM KULTURBESITZ (See Kunstgewerbemuseum)

STEDELIJK MUSEUM
Paulus Potterstraat 13
1071 CX Amsterdam
Holland

Gerrit Rietveld   Buffet; Berlin Chair

UNIVERSITY OF GLASGOW, MACKINTOSH MUSEUM
University of Glasgow
Glasgow
Scotland

Charles Rennie Mackintosh   Pink and White Chair; D.S. Collection

VICTORIA AND ALBERT MUSEUM
South Kensington
London SW7 2RL
U.K.

Ernest Gimson   Checkerboard Chest
Edward William Godwin   Sideboard; Chair
Arthur Heygate Mackmurdo   Chair
Peter Murdoch   Polka Dot Child's Chair
Makay Hugh Ballie Scott   Music Cabinet for Grand Duke of Hesse
Charles Francis Annesley Voysey   Chair
Philip Webb   Oak Cabinet; Morris Chair
Leonard F. Wyburd   Thebes Stool

SELECTED BIBLIOGRAPHY

BOOKS AND EXHIBITION CATALOGS

Alison, Filippo. *Charles Rennie Mackintosh as a Designer of Chairs*. Woodbury, N.Y.: Barron's, 1977.

Anscombe, Isabelle, and Charlotte Gere. *Arts and Crafts in Britain and America*. New York: Rizzoli, 1978.

Aronson, Joseph. *The Encyclopedia of Furniture*. New York: Crown Publishers, 1965.

Arwas, Victor. *Art Deco*. New York: Harry N. Abrams, Inc., 1980.

Ball, Victoria Kloss. *Architecture and Interior Design*. New York: John Wiley and Sons, Inc., 1980.

Baroni, Daniele. *Rietveld Furniture*. London: Barron, 1978.

Battersby, Martin. *Art Nouveau*. London: Colour Library of Art, 1969.

——. *The Decorative Thirties*. London: Studio Vista, 1971.

——. *The Decorative Twenties*. New York: Walker and Company, 1969.

——. *The History of Furniture*. New York: William Morrow & Co., Inc., 1976.

Bayer, Herbert, Walter Gropius, and Andise Gropius, eds. *Bauhaus: 1919–1928*. New York: The Museum of Modern Art, 1975.

Beer, Eileene Harrison. *Scandinavian Design: Objects of a Life Style*. New York: Farrar, Straus & Giroux and The American-Scandinavian Society, 1975.

Billcliffe, Roger. *Charles Rennie Mackintosh: The Complete Furniture, Furniture Drawings and Interior Design*. New York: Taplinger, 1979.

——. *Macintosh Furniture*. New York: E.P. Dutton & Co., 1985.

Bishop, Robert. *Centuries and Styles of the American Chair: 1640–1970*. New York: E.P. Dutton & Co., 1972.

Boger, Louise Ade. *Furniture Past & Present: A Complete Illustrated Guide to Furniture Styles from Ancient to Modern*. Garden City, N.Y.: Doubleday & Co., 1966.

Boyce, Charles. *Dictionary of Furniture*. New York: Facts on File, Inc., 1985.

Busch, Akiko, and Editors of Industrial Design Magazine, eds. *Product Design*. New York: PBC International, Inc., 1984.

Bush, Donald J. *Streamlined Decade: Design in the Nineteen Thirties*. New York: George Braziller, Inc., 1975.

Cathers, David M. *Furniture of the American Arts and Crafts Movement*. New York: New American Library, 1981.

Dalisi, Riccardo. *Gaudi: Furniture and Objects*. Woodbury, N.Y.: Barron's, 1979. Translated into English by Martha Boca.

Dexter, A. *Charles Eames: Furniture from the Design Collection*. New York: The Museum of Modern Art, 1973.

Domergue, Denise. *Artists Design Furniture*. New York: Harry N. Abrams, Inc., 1984.

Drexler, Arthur, and Greta Daniel. *Introduction to Twentieth-Century Design from the Collection of the Museum of Modern Art*. Garden City, N.Y.: Doubleday & Co., 1959.

Duncan, Alastair. *American Art Deco*. New York: Harry N. Abrams, Inc., 1986.

Emery, Marc. *Furniture by Architects*. New York: Harry N. Abrams, Inc., 1983.

Faulkner, Ray, Sarah Faulkner, and LuAnn Nissen. *Inside Today's Home*. 5th ed. New York: Holt, Rinehart and Winston, 1986.

Fleming, John, Hugh Honour. *Dictionary of the Decorative Arts*. New York: Harper & Row, 1977.

Frey, Gilbert. *The Modern Chair: 1850 to Today*. New York: Architectural Book Publishing Co., 1970.

Gandy, Charles D., and Susan Zimmermann-Stidham. *Contemporary Classics*. New York: McGraw-Hill Book Company, 1981.

Garner, Philippe. *Contemporary Decorative Arts*. New York: Facts on File, Inc., 1980.

——. *Phaidon Encyclopedia of Decorative Arts. 1890–1940*. Oxford: Phaidon Press Ltd., 1978.

——. *Twentieth-Century Furniture*. Oxford: Phaidon Press Ltd., 1980.

Grow, Lawrence. *Modern Style: A Catalogue of Contemporary Design*. Pittstown, N.J.: The Main Street Press, 1985.

Hanks, David A. *The Decorative Designs of Frank Lloyd Wright*. New York: E.P. Dutton & Co., 1979.

Hard af Segerstad, Ulf. *Modern Scandinavian Furniture*. Totowa, N.J.: Bedminster Press, 1963.

Harling, Robert. *Dictionary of Design and Decoration*. New York: Viking Press, 1973.

Harvey, Mary, Malcom Haslam, Philippe Garner, and Hugh Conway. *The Amazing Bugattis: Three Generations of Craftsmen, Artists & Designers*. Woodbury, N.Y.: Barron's Educational Series, Inc., 1979.

——. *High Styles: Twentieth Century American Design*. New York: Whitney Museum of American Art, 1985.

SELECTED BIBLIOGRAPHY

Howarth, Thomas. *Charles Rennie Mackintosh and the Modern Movement.* 2nd ed. London: Routledge & Kegan Paul, 1977. Reprint. New York: Garland Publishing, 1977.

Horn, Richard. *Memphis: Objects, Furniture, and Patterns.* Philadelphia: Running Press, 1985.

Humphries, Lund. *Modern Chairs: 1918–1970* Exhibition Catalogue. London: Whitechapel Art Gallery, 1970.

Kane, Patricia E. *300 Years of American Seating.* Boston: Little, Brown & Company, 1976.

Klein, Dan. *Art Deco.* New York: Crown Publishers, 1974.

——. *Furniture Design from Italy: Köln Stadt Museum Exhibit.* Rome: Istituto Nazionale per il Commercio Estero, 1980.

Kron, Joan, and Suzanne Slesin. *High-Tech: The Industrial Style and Source Book for the Home.* New York: Clarkson N. Porter, Inc., 1978.

Logie, Gordon. *Furniture from Machines.* London: George Allen & Unwin Ltd., 1974.

Lucie-Smith, Edward. *Furniture: A Concise History.* New York: Oxford University Press, 1979.

McClinton, Katharine Morrison. *Art Deco: A Guide for Collectors.* New York: Clarkson N. Potter, Inc./Publishers, 1972. Distributed by Crown Publishers.

Mackay, James. *Turn-of-the-Century Antiques: An Encyclopedia.* New York: E.P. Dutton & Co., Inc., 1974.

Makinson, Randell L. *Greene & Greene: Architecture as Fine Art.* Santa Barbara and Salt Lake City: Peregrine Smith, Inc., 1977.

Mang, Karl. *History of Modern Furniture.* New York: Harry N. Abrams, Inc., 1978.

Meadmore, Clement. *The Modern Chair: Classics in Production.* New York: Van Nostrand Reinhold Company, 1975.

——. *Mies van der Rohe: Exhibition Catalogue.* New York: The Museum of Modern Art, 1977.

Molesworth, H.D. and John Kenworthy-Browne. *Three Centuries of Furniture in Color.* New York: Viking Press, 1972.

Moller, S.E., ed. *Danish Design.* Copenhagen: Institute for Information, 1974.

Page, Marian. *Furniture Designed by Architects.* New York: Whitney Library of Design/Watson-Guptill, 1980.

Papachristow, Tician. *Marcel Breuer: New Buildings and Projects.* New York: Frederick A. Praeger, Inc., 1970.

Pevsner, Nikolaus. *Pioneers of Modern Design: From William Morris to Walter Gropius.* New York: Penguin Books, 1975.

——. *Post-Modern Classicism: The New Synthesis.* New York: Rizzoli, 1980.

Prete, Barbara, ed. *Chair.* New York: Thomas Y. Crowell, 1978.

Radice, Barbara. *Memphis: Ricerche, Esperienze, Risultati, Fallimenti e Successi del Nuovo Design.* Milan: Electa, 1984.

Raynsford, Julia. *The Story of Furniture.* London and New York: Hamlyn, 1975.

Russell, Frank, Philippe Garner, and John Read. *A Century of Chair Design.* New York: Rizzoli, 1980.

Selz, Peter, and Mildred Constantine, eds. *Art Nouveau: Art and Design at the Turn of the Century.* New York: The Museum of Modern Art, 1972.

Semback, Klaus-Jürgen, *Contemporary Furniture: An International Review of Modern Furniture, 1950 to the Present.* New York: Architectural Book Publishing Co., 1982.

Shaefer, Herwin. *Nineteenth Century Modern.* New York, 1970.

VanRensselaer, Mariana Griswold. *Henry Hobson Richardson and His Works.* New York: Dover Publications, Inc., 1969.

Waddell, Roberta. *The Art Nouveau Style.* New York: Dover Publications, Inc., 1977.

Warren, Geoffrey, *Art Nouveau Style.* London: Octopus, 1972.

Watson, Sir Francis. *The History of Furniture.* London: Orbio Publishing, 1982.

Weihsmann, Helmut. *Art Nouveau in Vienna.* Vienna: Ars Nova Media, 1983.

Whiton, Sherrill. *Elements of Interior Design.* 4th ed. New York: J.B. Lippincott Co., 1974.

Wilk, Christopher. *Marcel Breuer Furniture and Interiors.* New York: The Museum of Modern Art, 1981.

Windsor, Alan. *Peter Behrens: Architect and Designer 1868–1940.* New York: Whitney Library of Design/Watson-Guptill, 1981.

Young, Dennis and Barbara. *Furniture in Britain Today.* New York: Wittenborn and Company, 1964.

MAGAZINES AND JOURNALS

Abitaire
Abitare
Architectural Digest
Art News
Better Homes & Gardens
Casa Vogue
Contract
Design From Denmark
Design From Scandinavia
Design Quarterly
Designers West
Domus
House and Garden
Industrial Design
Interior Design
Interiors
Living Architecture: Scandinavian Design
Metropolis
Metropolitan Home
Mobilia
Rassegna
Smithsonian
Time
Woodworking & Furniture Digest

INDEX

AEO (Deganello), 155
AID (ASID) Design Award, 109, 120, 125, 126, 133, 148, 175
Aalto, Alvar, 65, 85, 90–92, 96, 98
Aarnio, Eero, 97, 109
Action Office System (Probst), 125
Additional System Lounge (Colombo), 134
Aesthetic Movement, 19
Albers, Josef, 60
Albini, Franco, 84, 130
Alias, 169
Allen, Davis, 176
Allen Table (Wright), 26
Aluminum Chair (Burton), 169
Aluminum Group (Breuer), 65
Aluminum Group Chair (Eames), 116
Ambiant Systems Ltd., 180
Andersson (AB Karl) & söner, 108
Andover Armchair (Allen), 176
Anfibio Sofa (Becchi), 154
Anglo-Japanese style, 19
Ant Chair (Jacobsen), 102
Antelope Chair (Race), 146
Appoggio Chair (Salocchi), 153
Architecture
    De Stijl, 56, 57
    organic, 22–23, 26
    Prairie School, 26, 28
Archizoom, 155, 178
Arconas Corp., 149
Arflex, 130
Argentina, 95
Argyle Chair (Mackintosh), 38
Argyle Set (Mackintosh), 38
Arkitektura, 82
Armchair 11 (Kjaerholm), 104
Armlöffel Chair (Hoffmann), 49
Art Deco, 51, 74–83, 84
Art et Industrie, 184
Art Furniture, 17, 19, 20, 22, 185
Art Institute of Chicago, The, 28
Art Nouveau, 20, 30–43, 53
Artek Company, 90, 91, 92, 98

Artemide, 132, 136, 153
Artifort, 147, 148, 149
Arts and Crafts Movement
    American, 22–23, 24–25, 29
    English, 16–21, 33
Arts of Denmark Exhibition of 1960, 88
Ascan Form, 172
Asko, 109
Asplund, Erik Gunnar, 85, 92, 93, 96
Asserbo Chair 504 (Mogensen), 108
Atelier International, 26, 27, 38, 39, 40, 57, 58, 70, 71, 92, 93, 94, 131, 140, 141, 155, 157, 178, 187
Atlantis Group (Castle), 174
Aulenti, Gae, 137, 161
Austria
    Bentwood, 12–13
    Vienna Secession, 46–48, 53
    Wiener Werkstätte, 45, 46–52, 53
Avarte, 110
Ax Chair (Hvidt), 99

BA Chair (Race), 146
B & B Italia, 139
B.D. Ediciones de Diseño, 36, 39, 40
B-9 Chair (Thonet), 13, 52, 71, 73, 121, 137, 171
Badovici, Jean, 83
Baillie Scott, Mackay Hugh, 33
Baker Furniture Company, 172
Baker, Knapp & Tubbs, 72
Bamburg Metallwerkstätten, 67
Barcelona Chair and Stool (Mies), 68
Barcelona Exhibition of 1929, 68, 177
Baresel-Bofinger, 144
Barrel Chair (Wright), 94
Basculant (LC-1) Chair (Le Corbusier), 70
Basile, Ernesto, 37
Basket Chair (Probber), 158
Bassett-Lowke, W.J., 41
Bastiano Sofa and Settee (Scarpa), 135
Baugham, Milo, 183
Bauhaus, 60–64, 67, 68

Becchi, Alessandro, 154
Behr 1600 Wall System (Lange), 144
Behrens, Peter, 44, 52
Belgium, 34
Bellato, 140
Bellinger, Gretchen, 94
Bellini, Mario, 140, 157, 163
Belotti, Giandomenico, 131
Bench with Horses (McKie), 165
Bennett, Ward, 162
Bentwood furniture
    Aalto, 90
    American, 24
    Hansen, 88
    Hoffmann, 48, 52
    steam process in, 10
    Thonet Industries, 12–13
    Wagner, 46
Berger, Veli, 160
Berlage, Hendrikus Petrus, 54, 56
Berlin Chair (Rietveld), 58
Berlin Exhibition of 1923, 58
Bertoia, Harry, 119
Bieffeplast, 95
Bikini Chair (Eames), 115
Bing, Samuel, 30, 34
Birds in Flight (Paulin), 149
Blow Chair (Scolari), 138
Blue Collection (Saarinen), 82
Bodyform Chair (Danko), 181
Boeri, Cini, 154
Bombé Chest, 79
Bonaventure Furniture Industries, 175
Bonet, Antonio, 15, 95
Botium, 111
Botta, Mario, 169
Bouloum (Mourgue), 149
Brazil, 142–43, 145
Breuer, Marcel, 55, 59, 60, 62–65, 85, 90, 158
Brickel Associates, 162
Brno Chair (Mies), 66
Brown Jordan, 120
Bugatti, Carlo, 37

INDEX

Burgasser, Joan, 159
Burne-Jones, Edward, 33
Burton, Scott, 169
Butterfly Chair (Hardoy, Bonet, and
    Kurchan), 15, 85, 95

Cab Chair (Bellini), 157
Cado, 108
Café Series (Pelikan Design), 171
California School, 23
Canada, 180
Cantilever chair, 55
    Aalto, 90, 92
    Breuer, 63
    Kjaerholm, 105
    Mies, 59, 64, 66, 67, 68
    Ostergaard, 108
    Panton, 106
    Stam, 59
    Tatlin, 73
Carlton (Sottass), 182
Cassina, 26, 27, 38, 39, 40, 41, 57, 58,
    59, 70, 71, 92, 93, 94, 131, 135,
    136, 140, 141, 155, 157, 161, 163,
    178, 186, 187
Castiglioni, Achille, 132, 152
Castiglioni, Pier Giacoma, 132
Castle, Wendell, 174
Cathedra Chair (Richardson), 24
Century Furniure, 179
Century Guild, 33
Cesca Chair (Breuer), 64, 158
Chadwick, Don, 160
Chadwick Modular Seating (Chadwick),
    160
Chair 20 (Kjaerholm), 105
Chair 22 (Kjaerholm), 104
Chair 24 (Wegner), 101
Chair 290 (Ostergaard), 108
Chair 300 (Paulin), 148
Chair 424 (Mascheroni), 127
Chair 506 (Harcourt), 147
Chair 577 (Paulin), 149
Chair 925 (Scarpa), 136
Chair 932/2 (Bellini), 140
Chair 4860 (Colombo), 141
Chaise Ronde (Studio/Alchymia), 182
Checkerboard Chest (Gimson), 21
Cherner, Norman, 121
Cheru Enterprises, 157

Chiavari Chair (Rambaldi), 86
Chiavari Workshop, 86
Chicago World Exhibition of 1893, 53
China Chair (Wegner), 100
Christiansen, Hans, 53
Citterio, 15
Classic Chair (Wegner), 101
Classic Modernism, 92, 175, 180
Club Tub (Burgasser), 159
Coconut Chair (Nelson), 113, 122
Coggin, Thayer, 183
Cole, Isaac, 24
Collinson & Lock, 33
Colombo, Joe, 133, 134, 141
Colonial Chair, 11, 14, 70
Comfort, Giorgetti Fratelli & Company,
    133
Comforto, 173
Compagnie des Arts Français, 78
Comprehensive Storage System (Nelson),
    123
Confort Chair (Le Corbusier), 70, 140
Cooper-Hewitt Museum, N.Y.C., 81,
    120
Copenhagen Cabinetmakers' Guild, 88,
    111
Copenhagen School of Arts and Crafts,
    101
Coray, Hans, 85, 95
Corbusier Chair. See B-9 Chair (Thonet)
Craft Revival Movement, 151, 164–65,
    166, 174
Craftsman, The, 23, 28
Craftsman Workshops, 25
Cranbrook Academy of Design, 43, 82,
    114, 119, 125
Cranston, Miss, 38, 40
Crate Furniture (Rietveld), 59
Cyma recta curves, 68

DAR Shell Chair (Eames), 115
DCW Molded Plywood Chair (Eames),
    114
DKR Chair (Eames), 115
D.S. Collection (Mackintosh), 41
DSI, 100, 101
Dahl, Per Kristian, 172
Dali, Salvador, 85, 87
Danko, Peter, 181
Danko (Peter) & Associates, 181

Danske Kunstindustrimuseet,
    Copenhagen, 34
Darmstadt Artists' Colony, 52, 53
Darmstadt style, 52, 53
Day, Robin, 146
De Fuccio, Robert, 159
De Pas, Jonathan, 138, 156
De Stijl, 55, 57
De Stijl Movement, 54–59, 60, 61,
    62–65
Deganello, Paolo, 155, 178
Denmark
    Danish Modern, 99–101, 103, 104
    Early Modern, 88, 89
    in 1980s, 170, 171, 172
    postwar, 99–108, 110–11
Design Studio, 139, 156
Deskey, Donald, 83
Deutscher Werkbund, 42, 44, 52
Deutscher Werkbund Exhibition of
    1927, 66, 92
Diffrient, Niels, 173
Doctor Sonderbar (Starck), 168
Domus, 84, 130
Dondolo Rocking Chair (Leonardi and
    Stagi), 140
Donghia, Angelo, 180
Donghia Furniture, 180
Doucet, Jacques, 80
du Pasquier, Nathalie, 183
D'Urbino, Donato, 138, 156
Ducrot, Vittorio, 37
Dunbar, 186
Dux Möbel, 98

Eames, Charles, 112, 114–17, 156
Eames, Ray Kaiser, 112, 114–17
Eames Chair, 116, 173
Eastlake, Charles, 17, 19, 20, 22
Easy Edges (Gehry), 157
Ebony Gothic Chair (Makepeace), 165
Ecart International, 56, 72
Eclipse Chair (Spectre), 179
Edison, Thomas, 15
Elda 1005 Chair (Colombo), 133
Ellis, Harvey, 25
Elmslie, George Grant, 23, 28, 29
England
    Art Nouveau, 33
    Arts and Crafts Movement, 16–21, 33

Craft Revival Movement, 164, 165
Early Modern, 89
International Style, 65
in nineteenth century, 14, 15
in 1930s, 89, 94
postwar, 143, 146–47
Ergonomics, 166–67, 173
Essex and Suffolk Insurance Company, 21
Evans Products Company, 114
L'Exposition des Arts Decoratifs of 1925, 74

Fenby, Joseph Beverly, 11, 15
Ferrieri, Anna Castelli, 153
Festival of Britain, 143, 146
Feure, Georges de, 34
50/Fifty, 121
Finland
    Early Modern, 90–92
    National Romantic Style, 43
    postwar, 98, 109–10
Fiorenza Chair (Albini), 130
Fledermaus Chair (Hoffmann), 49
Floating Dock (Utzon), 111
Forbes, Eleanor, 124
formes nouvelles, 72
Forum Furniture (Olsen and Dahl), 172
Four Seasons restaurant, N.Y.C., 66
France
    Art Deco, 76–80, 83
    Art Nouveau, 34–36
    International Style, 70–73, 83
    in 1980s, 168
    postwar, 143, 148–49
Frank, Jean-Michel, 80, 87
Frankl, Paul, 81
Frattini, Gianfranco, 135
Freideberg, Pedro, 143, 145
French Moderne. See Art Deco
Friedman (Barry), Ltd., 32, 35, 37, 46, 89, 98
Friedman, Stanley Jay, 175
Furniture of the Twentieth Century, 39, 40, 56, 65, 72, 86
Futurism, 84

GF 40/4 Chair (Rowland), 125
GF Furniture Systems, 125
Gallé, Emile, 35

Gallé-Kallela, Akseli, 43
Gamble House, Cal., 25
Gatti, Piero, 139, 156
Gaudí, Antonio, 36
Gaudi Chair (Magistretti), 153
Gavina, 65
Gehry, Frank O., 157
Gemeentemuseum, The Hague, 56
Genni Lounge Chair, 87
Germany
    Bauhaus, 60–64, 66, 67, 68
    Darmstadt style, 52, 53
    International Style, 63, 65, 66, 68, 69
    Jugendstil, 42
    Munich Secession, 52
    in 1970s, 158
    in 1980s, 172, 173
    postwar, 142, 144
Gesellius, Herman, 43
Gilardi, Piero, 138
Gimson, Ernest, 21
Giovannetti, 154
Glasgow/Art Nouveau, 38–41
Glasgow School of Art, 38, 39
Globe (Aarnio), 109
Godwin, Edward William, 19
Gold Medal Company, 15
Goldman, Paul, 121
Goteborg Chairs (Asplund), 92
Gothic/Romanesque style, 24
Grace, Thomas Lear, 182
Grace Designs, 182
Gragg, Samuel, 24
Grand Flute (Donghia), 180
Grand Rapids Art Museum, 81
Graves, Michael, 178
Gray, Eileen, 72, 76, 83
Greene, Charles Sumner, 23, 25
Greene, Henry Mather, 23, 25
Gregori, Bruno, 182
Gropius, Walter, 52, 60, 61, 62, 65, 85
Groult, André, 79
Group N, 139
Gruppo 7, 84, 86
Gufram, 138, 156
Gugelot, Hans, 112, 144
Guimard, Hector, 34, 36
Gullichsen, Mairea, 91
Gunlocke Company, The, 174
Guthrie and Wells, 39

Gwathmey, Charles, 179
Gyro Chair (Aarnio), 109

Hammock Chair 24 (Kjaerholm), 105
Hand Chair (Freideberg), 145
Hansen (Carl) & Son, 101
Hansen, Fritz, 88, 99, 100, 102, 103, 104, 105, 106, 107, 110, 111, 171
Hansen, Søren, 88
Harcourt, Geoffrey, 147
Hardoy, Jorge Ferrari, 15, 95
Harper, Irving, 122
Haugesen, Niels Jorgen, 170
Haus Koller Chair (Hoffmann), 51
Herbst, René, 72
Herman Miller, 112, 114, 115, 116, 117, 119, 121, 122, 123, 125, 160
Hesse, Grand Duke of, 33, 47
Highback Lounge Chair (Bertoia), 119
Hill House Chairs (Mackintosh), 39
Hints on Household Taste in Furniture, Upholstery, and Other Details (Eastlake), 17, 20
Hoffmann, Josef, 11, 44, 45, 46, 48–52, 176
Hoffmann Chair, 52
Hoffmann Rocking Chair, 48
Horn GmbH., 106
Horta, Victor, 32
Hubbard, Elbert, 22–23, 29
Hvidt, Peter, 96, 99
Hvidt and Mølgaard-Nielsen, 99
Hvitträsk, 43

ICF, 43, 48, 49, 50, 51, 64, 82, 87, 90, 91, 98, 120, 131, 132, 139, 152, 168, 169, 170, 179
IN50 Table (Noguchi), 119
IL Colonnato Tables (Bellini), 163
Illinois Institute of Technology, 67
Image, Selwyn, 33
Imperial Hotel Chair (Wright), 81
Ingram Street Chair (Mackintosh), 40
Inouye, Tadao E., 120
International Exhibition of 1862, 19
International Style, 60, 63, 65–66, 68–73, 76, 83
    reaction against, 84–85, 129
    in Scandinavia, 92, 93, 96
Ionic, The (Studio 65), 156

Iribe, Paul, 76, 80
Iris Company, 43
Isokon Lounge Chair (Breuer), 65
Italy
    Italian Modern, 130
    Early Modern, 86
    Memphis Design Group, 182
    Milan School, 130
    in 1970s, 152–57, 160, 161, 162,
      163
    in 1980s, 182, 186, 187
    postwar, 128–41, 145
    Rationalist Movement, 84, 86, 87
    Stile Liberty, 37

J.G. Furniture Systems, 72
JH 501 (Wegner), 101
JH 550 (Wegner), 100
Jacobsen, Arne, 96, 102, 103, 106, 110
Jalk, Grete, 103
Japan, 181, 187
Jeannert, Charles-Edouard. *See* Le
    Corbusier
Jeanneret, Pierre, 70, 71
Jefferson Chair (Diffrient), 173
Jeppesen (P.) Company, 103
Joe Lounge Chair (Design Studio), 156
Johnson, Philip, 66
Jordan-Volpe Gallery, N.Y.C., 25, 28, 29
Jugendstil, 30, 42
Juhl, Finn, 96, 98

Kandinsky, Wassily, 60
Kane, Brian, 175
Kantan Collection (Inouye), 120
Kartell, 133, 141, 153
Karuselli Chair (Kukkapuro), 110
Katavolos, William, 120
Kelly, Douglas, 120
Kinsman, Rodney, 95
Kips Bay Sofa (Saladino), 186
Kita, Toshiyuki, 187
Kjaerholm, Poul, 97, 104–5
Klee, Paul, 60
Klint, Kaare, 11, 14, 85, 89, 96, 108
Klismos Chair (Robsjohn-Gibbings), 94
Knoll International, 63, 65, 66, 67, 68,
    69, 95, 113, 118, 119, 126, 127,
    134, 135, 154, 159, 161, 177, 176,
    185

Koch, Mogens, 85, 88
Kohn, Jacob and Josef, 49
Kosuga & Company, 181
Kroin, 158
Krueger, 137, 148
Kubus Chair (Hoffmann), 50
Kukkapuro, Yrjö, 97, 110
Kukkasjarvi, Irma, 43, 82
Kunstgewerbemuseum Staatliche Museen
    Kultburbesitz, West Berlin, 42
Kurchan, Juan, 15, 95
Kurokawa, Kisho, 181

LCM Dining Chair (Eames), 114
LC-2 Petit Confort (Le Corbusier), 70,
    140
LC-4 (Le Corbusier), 71
LC-7 (Le Corbusier), 71
Lamb, Thomas, 180
Landi Stacking Chair (Coray), 95
Lange, Jürgen, 112, 144
Larsen, Henning, 110
Larsen, Jack Lenor, 42
Laurent, M., 77
Le Corbusier, 11, 13, 52, 70–71, 105
Legrain, Pierre, 80
Leisure Collection (Schultz), 126
Leleu, Jules-Emile, 79
Leonardi, Cesare, 140
Liberty, Arthur Lasenby, 20
Liberty & Company, 20, 33
Lindgren, Armas, 43
Littell, Ross, 120
Lomazzi, Paolo, 138, 156
London Exhibition of 1851, 10
Loos, Adolf, 44, 46, 47
Lorenz, Anton, 159
Lorry (Grace), 182
Lunario Table (Boeri), 154

M125 Modular Group (Gugelot), 144
MR Chair (Mies), 66, 67
MR Lounges (Mies), 67
Macdonald, Frances, 38
Macdonald, Margaret, 38, 49
McGuire, Eleanor, 124
McGuire Company, The, 124
McKie, Judy Kensley, 165
Mackintosh, Charles Rennie, 19, 31,
    38–41, 49, 77, 176

Mackmurdo, Arthur Heygate, 33
MacNair, Herbert, 38
Mae West Lips (Dali), 85, 87
Magistretti, Vico, 131, 132, 153, 155,
    187
Maher, George Washington, 23, 28
Maholy-Nagy, Lázlo, 60
Main, Terence and Laura, 184
Majorelle, Louis, 35
Makepeace, John, 165
Mallet-Stevens, Robert, 72, 73
Maloof, Sam, 164
Mangiarotti, Angelo, 162
Manhattan Suite (Siciliano), 185
Maralunga (Magistretti), 155
Mare, André, 78
Marilyn (Dali), 87
Marshmallow Sofa (Nelson), 113, 122
Mascheroni, John, 127
Mascheroni Designs, 127
Mathsson, Bruno, 85, 90, 96, 98, 173
Mazza, Sergio, 136, 153
Meda, Luca, 177
Meier, Richard, 176
Meister, Howard, 184
Memphis design group, 122, 152, 167,
    178, 182–83
Memphis Milano, 182, 183
Mendini, Allessandro, 182
Metropolitan Furniture Corp., 175
Metropolitan Museum of Art, N.Y.C.,
    77, 79
MEWA P + W Blattmann, 95
Mexico, 145
Mezzadro Tractor Seat (Castiglioni), 132
Midway Chair (Wright), 27
Midway Gardens project, 27
Mies van der Rohe, Ludwig, 52, 55, 59,
    60, 66–69, 105
Milan Furniture Fair 1961, 182
Milan International Furniture Exhibition
    1969, 136
Milan School, 130
Milan Triennale, 99, 104, 125, 129,
    130, 131, 136, 141, 146, 148
Mission Style, 23, 28, 29
Møbelsnedkeri, Johannes Hansen, 100,
    101
Mogensen, Børge, 96, 108
Model No. 14 Chair (Thonet), 12, 64

Modello 780 (Frattini), 135
Modern movement
  early, 10–15
  See also specific movements; names; styles
Modernismo, 30, 36
Molteni, 177
Mondrian, Piet, 54, 57
Monza Armchair (Terragni), 86
Monza Exhibition, 86
Morris, William, 16, 18, 22, 23, 28, 60
Morris Chair, 18
Morris, Marshall & Faulkner, 16
Moser, Koloman, 45, 46, 48, 53
Mourge, Olivier, 143, 149
Mucchi, Gabriele, 84, 87
Munich Secession, 42, 52
Murdoch, Peter, 147
Musée des Arts Décoratifs, Paris, 35, 36, 76, 77, 78, 80, 149
Museum für Kunst und Gewerbe, Hamburg, 43
Museum of Fine Arts, Boston, 24, 165
Museum of Modern Art, The, N.Y.C., 24, 27, 34, 62, 65, 106, 113, 114, 115, 120, 124, 125, 128, 132, 141, 146, 149, 157, 161, 180, 181, 186, 187
Mushroom Chair (Aarnio), 109
Muthesius, Hermann, 44

National Romantic Movement, 43
Nelson, George, 112–13, 114, 121, 122–23
Neo-Functionalism, 144
Netherlands
  De Stijl, 54–59
  Early Dutch Modern, 56, 59
Network Chair (Haugesen), 170
Nienkämper, 106
Nikol International/Delta Export, 73
Noguchi, Isamu, 119
Nonstop Sofa (Peduzzi-Riva), 160
Nordenfjeldske Kunstindustrimuseum, Trondheim, 32
Nothing Continues to Happen (Meister), 184

OCA, 145
Odessa (Belotti), 131
Offenburg Park Chair (Wirth), 158

Olbrich, Josef Maria, 45, 46, 47
Olivetti Synthesis, 152
Olsen, Stig Herman, 172
Omkstack sheet metal chair (Kinsman), 95
Ostergaard, Steen, 97, 108
Oud, J.J.P., 54, 56
Oxford Collection (Jacobsen), 103

Paimio Chair (Aalto), 90
Palais Stoclet, Brussels, 45
  Hoffmann chair, 50
Pankok, Bernhard, 42
Panton, Verner, 97, 106–7, 113
Panton Stacking Chair, 106
Panton System 1-2-3, 107
Pantonova Wire Furniture, 106
Paolini, Cesare, 139, 156
Paulin, Pierre, 148, 149
Paris Exhibition of 1925, 13, 79, 81
Paris Exposition of 1900, 34
Paris Métro entrances, 36
Parsons Table (Frank), 80
Pastilli Chair (Aarnio), 109
Peacock Chair (Wegner), 100
Peduzzi-Riva, Eleonore, 160
Pelikan Design, 171
Pension Armchair (Aalto), 90
Perriand, Charlotte, 70, 71
Pesce, Gaetano, 139, 161, 186
Pile, John, 121
Piretti, Giancarlo, 137
Platner, Warren, 126
Please Be Seated show, 120
Plia Chair (Piretti), 137
Plycraft, 121
Plywood bent design
  Breuer, 65
  Danko, 181
  Eames, 112, 114
  Summers, 89
Polka Dot Chair (Murdoch), 147
Pollock, Charles, 127
Poltronova, 156
Polyprop Chair (Day), 146
Ponti, Gio, 84, 130
Pony Chaise Lounge (Le Corbusier), 71, 105
Pop Art furniture, 85, 87, 145, 156
Porsche, Alexander Ferdinand, 72

Post-International Style, 142–43, 144, 148
Post-Modern, 178, 179, 185
Postal Savings Bank furniture (Wagner), 46
Prague Chair (Hoffmann), 52
Prairie School, 23, 26–29
Primate Kneeling Stool (Castiglione), 152
Prisma (Baughman), 183
Probber, Harvey, 158
Probst, Robert L., 125
Prussian Academy, Berlin, 52
Pugin, A.W.N., 22
Purcell, William Gray, 29
Purkersdorf Chair (Moser), 48

Queen Anne, Queen Anne (Main), 184

Race, Ernest, 143, 146
Radio City Music Hall, N.Y.C., 83
Rambaldi, Emanuele, 84, 86
Rattan OH-9 Officer's Chair (Forbes), 124
Red/Blue Chair (Rietveld), 57
Reich, Lilly, 68
Riart, Carlos, 177
Ribbon Chair (Paulin), 148
Richard III (Starck), 168
Richardson, Henry Hobson, 22, 24, 25
Riemerschmid, Richard, 42, 44
Rietveld, Gerrit, 54, 57–59, 106
Robie Chair (Wright), 26
Robie House, Chicago, 26
Robsjohn-Gibbings, T. H., 85, 94
Rock 'N' Roll Chair (Aarnio), 109
Rocking Chair (Riart), 177
Rocks (Gilardi), 138
Rockwell Chair (Goldman), 121
Rodriguez, Sergio, 142–43, 145
Roosevelt, Theodore, 15
Rossi, Aldo, 177
Rousseau, Clément, 78
Rowland, David, 125, 170
Royal Chaise (du Pasquier), 183
Roycrafter furniture, 29
Rubber Chair (Kane), 175
Rud. Rasmussens Snedkerier, 14, 88, 89, 107
Rudd International, 100, 102, 103, 104, 105, 110, 171
Ruhlmann, Jacques-Emile, 77

Ruskin, John, 16
Russian Constructivist School, 73, 80

S33 Chair (Stam), 59, 63
Saarinen, Eero, 112, 114, 118
Saarinen, Eliel, 43, 82
Sacco (Design Studio), 139
Safari Chair
    Klint, 11, 14
    Koch, 88
Saladino, John F., 186
Salocchi, Claudia, 153
Salone del Mobile Italiano, 129
Sapper, Richard, 173
Saridis of Athens, 94
Sassi (Gilardi), 138
Scarpa, Afra, 135, 136, 141
Scarpa, Tobia, 135, 136, 141
School of Nancy, France, 35
Schröder Table (Rietveld), 58
Schultz, Richard, 126
Scolari, 138
Scotland, 38–41
Secession Gallery, 45, 47
Seconda Armchair (Botta), 169
Selene Stacking Chair (Magistretti), 132
Sella cirulis stool, 68
Senna Chair (Asplund), 92
Serie Edo Chair (Kurokawa), 181
Series Up (Pesce), 139, 161
Series Sit-Down (Pesce), 161
Serpent Chair (Gray), 76

Shaker furniture, 11, 13, 61, 130
Shaw, Richard Norman, 22
Sheriff Chair (Rodriguez), 142–43, 145
Siciliano, Frank, 185
Siège Tournant Chair (Le Corbusier,
    Jeanneret, and Perriand), 71
Siegel, Gustav, 46
Siegel, Robert, 179
Silsbee, Joseph Lyman, 29
Sitzmachine, 48
Skipper Italy, 162
Sling Sofa (Nelson), 123
Société van de Velde, 32
Sof-Tech Collection (Rowland), 170
Solus (Aulenti), 137
Sorensen, Johnny, 111
Soriana Group (Scarpa), 141
Sormani, 134, 153
Sottsass, Ettore, Jr., 152, 182
Source One, 146
Spaghetti Chair (Belotti), 131
Spain, 36, 87, 177
Sparre, Louis, 43
Spectre, Jay, 179
Spoleto Chair (Breuer), 63
Spooks, The, 38
Spring Leaf Chair (Aalto), 92
Stacking Storage Thing (Ferrieri), 153
Stagi, Franca, 140
Stam, Mart, 11, 55, 59, 63, 64
Starck, Philippe, 168
Steamer Collection (Lamb), 180

Stedelijk Museum, Amsterdam, 57, 58
Stendig International, 83, 87, 160, 176
Stickley, Gustav, 22–23, 25, 28
Stile Liberty, 20, 30, 37
Stock Exchange Building, Amsterdam, 56
Stow/Davis, 159
Studio Alchymia, 182
Studio 65, Milan, 87, 156
Style Guimard, 36
Süe, Louis, 78
Sullivan, Louis, 29, 61
Summers, Gerald, 85, 89
SunarHauserman, 173, 178
Sunburst Chair (Rousseau), 78
Superleggera Chair (Ponti), 130
Surrealism, 87, 145
Suzanne Lounge Chair (Takahama), 134
Swan and Egg (Jacobsen), 102
Sweden
    Classic Modernism, 92
    International Style, 93
    Swedish Modern, 98
Swiss National Exhibition of 1938, 95
Switzerland, 95, 106, 107, 160, 169
Swivel Armchair (Pollock), 127
System 25 (Sapper), 173

T-Chair (Katavolos, Littell, and Kelly),
    120, 162
Takahama, Kazuhide, 134
Tandem Sling Seating System (Eames),
    117

Tassel House, 32
Tatlin, Vladimir, 73
Teak Style, 96
Teatro (Rossi and Meda), 177
Teodoro, Franco, 139, 156
Terragni, Giuseppe, 84, 86
Thebes Stool (Wyburd), 20
Thonet, Michael, 10, 12, 24, 64
Thonet Industries, 11, 12, 13, 46, 52,
    59, 64, 67, 71, 127, 137, 159, 170
3 Tre Chair (Mangiarotti), 162
Thygesen, Rud, 111
Tiffany, Louis, 53
Toga Chair (Mazza), 136, 153
Torso (Deganello), 178
Tramanto a New York (Pesce), 186
Transat Chair (Gray), 72
Triangle Chair (De Fuccio), 159
Tripolina Chair (Fenby), 11, 15, 95
Tubo Table (Mascheroni), 127
Tugendhat Chair (Mies), 68, 105
Tugendhat Table (Mies), 69
Tulip Pedestal Group (Saarinen), 118
Turin Exhibition of 1902, 37

Ulrich, Heinz, 160
Union des Artistes Modernes, 72, 73
United States
    Art Deco, 81–83
    Arts and Crafts Movement, 22–23,
        24–25, 29
    Classic Modernism, 175, 180

Craft Revival Movement, 164, 165,
    174
early modernism in, 22–29
Ergonomics, 173
in 1930s, 94
in 1970s, 157, 158–60, 162, 164,
    165
in 1980s, 169, 170, 173, 174,
    175–76, 178, 179–86
Post-Modern, 178, 179, 185
postwar, 112–27
Prairie School, 23, 27–29
Shaker furniture, 13
University Chair (Bennett), 162
University of Glasgow, 39, 41
Urban, Josef, 53
USSR, Russian Constructivist School in,
    73, 80
Utzon, Jørn, 97, 110, 111

van de Velde, Henri, 32, 60
van Doesburg, Theo, 54
Venice Biennale, 177
Venturi, Robert, 185
Veranda (Magistretti), 187
Victoria and Albert Museum, London,
    18, 19, 20, 21, 33, 88, 111, 147,
    161
Vienna Secession Movement, 31, 44–45,
    46–48, 52–53
Vienna Workshop. See Wiener Werkstätte
Villa Gallia Sofa (Hoffmann), 51

Vodder, Niels, 99
Vogt, Klaus, 160
Voysey, Charles Francis Annesley, 21

Wagner, Otto, 11, 44, 46
Wassily Chair (Breuer), 63, 70, 90
Webb, Philip, 18
Wegner, Hans, 42, 96, 100–101
Whistler, James McNeill, 39
White, John, 33
White Collection (Saarinen), 43
Wiener Werkstätte, 31, 45, 46–53
Williamson, Rupert, 164
Willow I (Mackintosh), 40
Willow (W-5) Chair (McGuire), 124
Windmill Furniture, 65
Wingspread House, Wisc., 94
Wire Collection (Platner), 126
Wirth, Heinz, 158
Wishbone Chair (Wegner), 101
Wink Chair (Kita), 187
Womb Chair (Saarinen), 118
World Exhibition of 1904, 42
Wright, Frank Lloyd, 19, 23, 26–27,
    28, 61, 81, 94
Wright Home and Studio Foundation, 26
Wyburd, Leonard, 20

Zabro, 182
Zanotta, 86, 87, 137, 138, 139
Zanuso, Marco, 133, 163
Zigzag Chair (Rietveld), 58, 106

CREDITS

THE BEGINNING OF MODERNISM
PAGES 10–11 *left to right* Thonet Industries, Inc.; Thonet Industries, Inc.; Tina McKnelly Jackson; Tina McKnelly Jackson; Thonet Industries, Inc.; Rud. Rasmussens Snedkerier (Louis Schnakenburg, photographer). **PAGE 12** *left* Thonet Industries, Inc. *right* Thonet Industries, Inc. **PAGE 13** *left* Thonet Industries, Inc. **PAGE 14** Rud. Rasmussens Snedkerier (Louis Schnakenburg, photographer). **PAGE 15** Citterio S.p.A.

ARTS AND CRAFTS MOVEMENT
PAGES 16–17 *left to right* Victoria and Albert Museum, London; Sally Sharpe; Victoria and Albert Museum, London; Tina McKnelly Jackson; Victoria and Albert Museum, London; Victoria and Albert Museum, London. **PAGE 18** *top* Victoria and Albert Museum, London. **PAGE 19** *left* Victoria and Albert Museum, London *right* Victoria and Albert Museum, London. **PAGE 20** *bottom* Victoria and Albert Museum, London. **PAGE 21** *right* Victoria and Albert Museum, London.

EARLY MODERNISM IN THE UNITED STATES
PAGES 22–23 *left to right* Museum of Fine Arts, Boston, gift of the Church of the Unity-Unitarian Universalist; Jordan-Volpe Gallery, New York; Collection, Gamble House, Pasadena, California (Marvin Rand, photographer); Collection, The Museum of Modern Art, New York, gift of Edgar Kaufmann Jr.; Atelier International, Ltd.; Jordan-Volpe Gallery, New York; Tina McKnelly Jackson. **PAGE 24** *left* Museum of Fine Arts, Boston, gift of the Church of the Unity-Unitarian Universalist *right* Collection, The Museum of Modern Art, New York, purchase. **PAGE 25** *left* Jordan-Volpe Gallery, New York *right* Collection, Gamble House, Pasadena, California (Marvin Rand, photographer). **PAGE 26** *top* Collection, Frank Lloyd Wright Home and Studio Foundation, Oak Park, Illinois *bottom* Atelier International, Ltd. **PAGE 27** *left* Collection, The Museum of Modern Art, New York, gift of Edgar Kaufmann Jr. *right* Atelier International, Ltd. **PAGE 28** *top* Jordan-Volpe Gallery, New York (Scott Hyde, photographer) *bottom* Collection, The Art Institute of Chicago, Robert R. McCormick Charitable Trust, 1983. **PAGE 29** *right* Jordan-Volpe Gallery, New York.

ART NOUVEAU
PAGES 30–31 *left to right* Collection, Nordenfjeldske Kunstindustrimuseum (Svein Lian, photographer); Collection, Victoria and Albert Museum, London; Collection, Danske Kunstindustrimuseet, Copenhagen (© Copyright Ole Woledbye); Collection, Musée des Arts Décoratifs, Paris; Cassina S.p.A. (Mario Carrieri, photographer); Cassina S.p.A. **PAGE 32** *left* Collection, Nordenfjeldske Kunstrindustrimuseum (Svein Lian, photographer) *right* Collection, Barry Friedman Ltd., New York (Stuart Friedman, photographer). **PAGE 33** *left* Collection, Victoria and Albert Museum, London. **PAGE 34** *top* Collection, Danske Kunstindustrimuseet, Copenhagen (© Copyright Ole Woledbye) *bottom* Collection, The Museum of Modern Art, New York, gift of Madame Hector Guimard. **PAGE 35** *left* Collection, Barry Friedman Ltd., New York (Stuart Friedman, photographer), lent by Museum of Art, Carnegie Institute, Pittsburgh *right* Collection, Musée des Arts Décoratifs, Paris. **PAGE 36** *left* Collection, Musée des Arts Décoratifs, Paris *right* B. D. Ediciones de Diseño. **PAGE 37** *right* Collection, Barry Friedman Ltd., New York (Stuart Friedman, photographer). **PAGE 38** *left* Cassina S.p.A. (Mario Carrieri, photographer) *right* Cassina S.p.A. (Mario Carrieri, photographer). **PAGE 39** *left to right* Tina McKnelly Jackson; Cassina S.p.A. (Mario Carrieri, photographer); Furniture of the Twentieth Century. **PAGE 40** *left* Cassina S.p.A. *right* Furniture of the Twentieth Century. **PAGE 41** Cassina S.p.A. (Mario Carrieri, photographer). **PAGE 42** *left* Jack Lenor Larsen *right* Collection, Kunstgewerbemuseum Staatliche Museen Kulturbesitz, West Berlin. **PAGE 43** *left* Collection, Museum für Kunst und Gewerbe, Hamburg (Kunstgewerbemuseum, Staatliche Museen PreuBischer Kulturbesitz, West Berlin) *right* ICF, Inc.

VIENNA SECESSION, WIENER WERKSTÄTTE, DEUTSCHER WERKBUND
PAGES 44–45 *left to right* Tina McKnelly Jackson; ICF, Inc.; Collection, Barry Friedman Ltd., New York; ICF, Inc.; ICF, Inc.; Tina McKnelly Jackson. **PAGE 46** *left* Collection, Bary Friedman Ltd., New York (Stuart Friedman, photographer) *right* Thonet Industries, Inc. **PAGE 48** *left* ICF, Inc. *right* ICF, Inc. **PAGE 49** *left* ICF, Inc. *right* ICF, Inc. **PAGE 50** *left* ICF, Inc. *right* ICF, Inc. **PAGE 51** *left* ICF, Inc. *right* ICF, Inc. **PAGE 52** *left* Thonet Industries, Inc.

MODERNISM IN HOLLAND
PAGES 54–55 *left to right* Furniture of the Twentieth Century; Atelier International, Ltd.; Collection, Stedelijk Museum,

Amsterdam; Atelier International, Ltd.; Atelier International, Ltd.; Cassina S.p.A. (Mario Carrieri, photographer). **PAGE 56** *right* Furniture of the Twentieth Century. **PAGE 57** *left* Atelier International, Ltd. *right* Collection, Stedelijk Museum, Amsterdam. **PAGE 58** *left to right* Collection, Stedelijk Museum, Amsterdam; Atelier International, Ltd.; Atelier International, Ltd. **PAGE 59** *top* Cassina S.p.A. (Mario Carrieri, photographer).

INTERNATIONAL STYLE AND BAUHAUS
PAGES 60–61 *left to right* Knoll International (Mikio Sekita, photographer); Thonet Industries, Inc.; Knoll International (Mikio Sekita, photographer); Knoll International (Mikio Sekita, photographer); Atelier International, Ltd.; Furniture of the Twentieth Century. **PAGE 62** *right* Collection, The Museum of Modern Art, New York, Phyllis B. Lambert Fund. **PAGE 63** *left* Knoll International (Mikio Sekita, photographer) *right* Knoll International. **PAGE 64** *left* Thonet Industries, Inc. *right* ICF, Inc. **PAGE 65** *left* Collection, The Museum of Modern Art, New York, gift of the designer *right* Furniture of the Twentieth Century. **PAGE 66** *top* Knoll International (Mikio Sekita, photographer) *bottom* Knoll International (Mikio Sekita, photographer). **PAGE 67** Knoll International (Mikio Sekita, photographer). **PAGE 68** *left* Knoll International (Mikio Sekita, photographer) *right* Knoll International. **PAGE 69** Knoll International (Mikio Sekita, photographer). **PAGE 70** *left* Atelier International, Ltd. *right* Atelier International, Ltd. **PAGE 71** *left* Atelier International, Ltd. *right* Atelier Inter-national, Ltd. **PAGE 72** *left* Furniture of the Twentieth Century *right* J. G. Furniture Systems. **PAGE 73** *left* Furniture of the Twentieth Century.

ART DECO
PAGES 74–75 *left to right* Collection, Musée des Arts Décoratifs, Paris; Collection, Musée des Arts Décoratifs, Paris; Collection, Musée des Arts Décoratifs, Paris; Collection, Musée des Arts Décoratifs, Paris; ICF, Inc. **PAGE 76** *left* Collection, Musée des Arts Décoratifs, Paris. **PAGE 77** *left* Collection, The Metropolitan Museum of Art, New York, bequest of Collis P. Huntington, 1973 *right* Collection, Musée des Arts Décoratifs, Paris. **PAGE 78** *left* Collection, Musée des Arts Décoratifs, Paris. **PAGE 79** *right* Collection, The Metropolitan Museum of Art, New York, gift of Miss Agnes Miles Carpenter, 1946. **PAGE 80** *bottom* Collection, Musée des Arts Décoratifs, Paris. **PAGE 81** *left* Courtesy of Cooper-Hewitt Museum, The Smithsonian Institution's National Museum of Design *right* Collection, Grand Rapids Art Museum, gift of Dr. and Mrs. John Halick (Mark A. Deremo, photographer). **PAGE 82** *top* ICF, Inc. *bottom* Arkitektura (Balthazar Korab, photographer). **PAGE 83** *left* Stendig International Inc.

THE 1930s
PAGES 84–85 *left to right* ICF, Inc.; Collection, Barry Friedman Ltd., New York (Stuart Friedman, photographer); ICF, Inc.; Cassina S.p.A. (Mario Carrieri, photographer); Gretchen Bellinger Inc. (Bill Kontzias, photographer); Atelier International, Ltd. **PAGE 86** *left* Furniture of the Twentieth Century. **PAGE 87** *top* ICF, Inc. *bottom* Stendig International Inc. **PAGE 89** *bottom* Collection, Barry Friedman Ltd., New York (Stuart Friedman, photographer). **PAGE 90** *left* ICF, Inc. *right* ICF, Inc. **PAGE 91** *left* ICF, Inc. *right* ICF, Inc. **PAGE 92** *left* ICF, Inc. *right* ICF, Inc. **PAGE 93** Cassina, S.p.A. (Mario Carrieri, photographer). **PAGE 94** *left* Gretchen Bellinger Inc. (Bill Kontzias, photographer) *right* Atelier International, Ltd. **PAGE 95** *bottom* MEWA P + W Blattmann (Hans Langendorf, photographer).

POSTWAR SCANDINAVIA
PAGES 96–97 *left to right* Collection, Barry Friedman Ltd., New York (Stuart Friedman, photographer); Fritz Hansen, Denmark (Schnakenburg & Brahl, photographer); Fritz Hansen, Denmark; Fritz Hansen, Denmark (Strüwing Reklamefoto); Fritz Hansen, Denmark; Nienkämper. **PAGE 98** *top* Collection, Barry Friedman Ltd., New York *bottom* ICF, Inc. **PAGE 99** *right* Fritz Hansen, Denmark. **PAGE 100** *left* Fritz Hansen, Denmark (Schnakenburg & Brahl, photographer) *right* Johannes Hansens Møbelsnedkeri (Schnakenburg & Brahl, photographer). **PAGE 101** *left* Johannes Hansens Møbelsnedkeri *right* Carl Hansen and Son (Schnakenburg & Brahl, photographer). **PAGE 102** *left* Fritz Hansen, Denmark *right* Fritz Hansen, Denmark (Strüwing Reklamefoto). **PAGE 103** *top* Fritz Hansen, Denmark. **PAGE 104** *left* Fritz Hansen, Denmark (Strüwing Reklamefoto) *right* Fritz Hansen, Denmark. **PAGE 105** *top* Fritz Hansen, Denmark (Strüwing Reklamefoto) *bottom* Fritz Hansen, Denmark (Strüwing Reklamefoto). **PAGE 106** *left* Nienkämper *right* Panton Design. **PAGE 107** Fritz Hansen, Denmark.

CREDITS

PAGE 108 *left* AB Karl Andersson & söner *right* Cado. PAGE 109 *left to right* Stendig International Inc.; Asko Oy; Asko Oy. PAGE 110 *left* Avarte Oy *right* Fritz Hansen, Denmark. PAGE 111 *top* Fritz Hansen, Denmark *bottom* Botium (Schnakenburg & Brahl, photographer).

POSTWAR AMERICA
PAGES 112–113 *left to right* Herman Miller Archives; Knoll International (Mikio Sekita, photographer); Herman Miller Archives; Knoll International (Mikio Sekita, photographer); Herman Miller Archives; GF Furniture Systems, Inc. PAGE 114 *left* Herman Miller Archives *right* Herman Miller Archives. PAGE 115 *left* Herman Miller Archives *right* Herman Miller Archives. PAGE 116 *left* Herman Miller Archives *right* Herman Miller Archives. PAGE 117 *top* Herman Miller Archives *bottom* Herman Miller Archives. PAGE 118 *top* Knoll International (Mikio Sekita, photographer) *bottom* Knoll International. PAGE 119 *top* Herman Miller Archives *bottom* Knoll International (Mikio Sekita, photographer). PAGE 120 *right* Brown Jordan. PAGE 121

left to right Herman Miller Archives; 50/Fifty (Michael Norgart, photographer); Plycraft, Inc. PAGE 122 *left* Herman Miller Archives *right* Herman Miller Archives. PAGE 123 *top* Herman Miller Archives *bottom* Herman Miller Archives. PAGE 124 *left* The McGuire Company *right* The McGuire Company. PAGE 125 *top* Herman Miller Archives *bottom* GF Furniture Systems, Inc. PAGE 126 *top* Knoll International *bottom* Knoll International. PAGE 127 *top* Knoll International (Mikio Sekita, photographer) *bottom* Mascheroni Designs.

POSTWAR ITALY
PAGES 128–129 *left to right* Arflex S.p.A. (Aldo Ballo, photographer); ICF, Inc.; Cassina S.p.A. (Aldo Ballo, photographer); Collection, Philadelphia Museum of Art (Eric E. Mitchell, photographer); Comfort, Cassina S.p.A. (Aldo Ballo, photographer). PAGE 130 *left* Arflex S.p.A. (Aldo Ballo, photographer) *right* Cassina S.p.A. (Aldo Ballo, photographer). PAGE 131 *left* ICF, Inc. *right* Cassina S.p.A. (Aldo Ballo, photographer). PAGE 132 *left* ICF, Inc. *right* Artemide

Inc. (Aldo Ballo, photographer). PAGE 133 *left* Collection, Philadelphia Museum of Art (Eric E. Mitchell, photographer) *right* Comfort. PAGE 134 *top* Knoll International (Mikio Sekita, photographer) *bottom* Arch. Ignazia Favata, Studio Joe Colombo, Milano (Fotografo Clari, Milano). PAGE 135 *top* Knoll International *bottom* Cassina S.p.A. (Aldo Ballo, photographer). PAGE 136 *left* Cassina S.p.A. PAGE 137 *left* Zanotta S.p.A. (Masera, Milano, photographer) *right* Krueger. PAGE 138 *top* Gufram *bottom* Zanotta S.p.A. (Masera, Milano, photographer). PAGE 139 *top* Zanotta S.p.A. (Masera, Milano, photographer) *bottom* B&B Italia S.p.A. PAGE 140 *left* Cassina S.p.A. (Aldo Ballo, photographer). PAGE 141 *top* Kartell *bottom* Atelier International, Ltd.

POSTWAR GERMANY, FRANCE, ENGLAND, BRAZIL, MEXICO
PAGES 142–143 *left to right* Tina McKnelly Jackson; Sally Sharp; Sally Sharp; Artifort; Artifort; Artifort. PAGE 144 *top* Bofinger Produktion, West Germany. PAGE 147 *top* Victoria and Albert Muse-

um, London *bottom* Artifort. **PAGE 148** *top* Artifort *bottom* Artifort. **PAGE 149** *left* Artifort *right* Arconas Corporation.

THE 1970s

PAGES 150–151 *left to right* Sormani S.p.A.; Atelier International, Ltd.; Gufram; Frank O. Gehry & Associates, Inc.; Brickel Associates Inc. (Stephen Ogilvy, photographer); Sam Maloof Studio (Jonathan Pollock, photographer). **PAGE 152** *left* ICF, Inc. *right* Olivetti Synthesis S.p.A. **Page 153** *left to right* Artemide Inc. (Aldo Ballo, photographer); Kartell (Centrokappa, photographer); Sormani S.p.A. **PAGE 154** *left* ICF, Inc. *right* Knoll International. **PAGE 155** *left* Atelier International, Ltd. *right* Cassina S.p.A. (Aldo Ballo, photographer). **PAGE 156** *top* Stendig International Inc. *bottom* Gufram. **PAGE 157** *left* Frank O. Gehry & Associates, Inc. *right* Atelier International, Ltd. (Aldo Ballo, photographer). **PAGE 158** *left* Kroin Inc. *right* Harvey Probber, Inc. **PAGE 159** *left* Thonet Industries, Inc. *right* Stow & Davis, a division of Steelcase Inc. **PAGE 160** *top* Stendig

International Inc. *bottom* Herman Miller Archives. **PAGE 161** *top* Cassina S.p.A. (Aldo Ballo, photographer) *bottom* Knoll International (Mikio Sekita, photographer). **PAGE 162** *left* Brickel Associates Inc. (Stephen Ogilvy, photographer) *right* Skipper Italy. **PAGE 163** Cassina S.p.A. (Aldo Ballo, photographer). **PAGE 164** *left* Sam Maloof Studio (Jonathan Pollock, photographer). **PAGE 165** *right* Collection, Museum of Fine Arts, Boston, purchased through funds provided by the National Endowment for the Arts and the Deborah M. Noonan Foundation.

THE 1980s

PAGES 166–167 *left to right* ICF, Inc.; SunarHauserman; Stendig International Inc.; Grace Designs; ICF, Inc.; Frank Siciliano. **PAGE 168** ICF, Inc. **PAGE 169** *top* ICF, Inc. *bottom* Max Protetch Gallery, collection Raymond Learsy, New York. **PAGE 170** *left* Thonet Indutries, Inc. *right* ICF, Inc. **PAGE 171** Fritz Hansen, Denmark. **PAGE 172** *left* Baker Furniture Company, Aves Advertising, Inc. *right* Ascan Form. **PAGE 173** *top* Comforto *bottom* SunarHauserman. **PAGE 174** The

Gunlocke Company. **PAGE 175** *left* Bonaventure Furniture Industries *right* Metropolitan Furniture Corporation (Burns and Associates, photographer). **PAGE 176** *left* Stendig International Inc. *right* Knoll International (Mikio Sekita, photographer). **PAGE 177** *left* Grace Designs *right* Knoll International (Mario Carrieri, photographer). **PAGE 178** *left* SunarHauserman *right* Atelier International, Ltd. **PAGE 179** *left* ICF, Inc. *right* Century Furniture Company. **PAGE 180** *left* Ambiant Systems Ltd. *right* Donghia Furniture Company. **PAGE 181** *left* Kosuga & Company *right* Peter Danko & Associates (© Copyright David Sharpe, photographer). **PAGE 182** *left to right* Grace Designs; Watson/Hague/Einstein, Inc.; Grace Designs. **PAGE 183** *top* Grace Designs *bottom* Thayer Coggin, Inc. **PAGE 184** *left* Art et Industrie *right* Art et Industrie. **PAGE 185** *left* Knoll International (Mario Carrieri, photographer) *right* Frank Siciliano. **PAGE 186** *top* Cassina S.p.A. (Mario Carrieri, photographer) *bottom* Dunbar. **PAGE 187** *left* Atelier International, Ltd. *right* Atelier International, Ltd.

Miriam Stimpson is a widely published author, a design consultant, and a teacher of interior design and the history of modern architecture. She has been a member of the Department of Design at Brigham Young University since 1972 and is an educational affiliate of the American Society of Interior Designers (ASID).

Stimpson resides in Provo, Utah, with her husband and four children.

FRONT COVER: Eliel Saarinen. Side Chair, Arkitektura, Inc. (Balthazar Korab, photographer).

BACK COVER *(counterclockwise from top left):* Michael Thonet. Chair No. 14, Thonet Industries, Inc.; Edward William Godwin. Chair, Victoria and Albert Museum, London; Georges de Feure. Sofa for the Paris Exposition, Collection, Danske Kunstindustrimuseet, Copenhagen (© Copyright Ole Woledbye); Otto Wagner. Postal Savings Bank Stool, Thonet Industries, Inc.; Le Corbusier. LC-4 Chaise Lounge, Atelier International, Ltd.; Charles and Ray Eames. Eames® DAR Shell Chair, Herman Miller Archives; Mario Bellini. IL Colonnato Table, Cassina S.p.A. (Aldo Ballo, photographer); Ettore Sottsass Jr. Carlton, Grace Designs.

SENIOR EDITOR: Julia Moore
ASSOCIATE EDITOR: Victoria Craven-Cohn
RESEARCH EDITOR: Linda Epstein
DESIGNER: Areta Buk
PRODUCTION MANAGER: Hector Campbell
Set in 11-point Caslon Old Face